Horizon

JULY, 1962 · *VOLUME IV, NUMBER 6*

HORIZON

A Magazine of the Arts

JULY, 1962 · *VOLUME IV, NUMBER 6*

PUBLISHER
James Parton

EDITORIAL DIRECTOR
Joseph J. Thorndike, Jr.

EDITOR
William Harlan Hale
MANAGING EDITOR
Eric Larrabee
ASSOCIATE EDITOR
Ralph Backlund
ASSISTANT EDITORS
Ada Pesin
Jane Wilson
Albert Bermel
CONTRIBUTING EDITOR
Margery Darrell
EDITORIAL ASSISTANTS
Shirley Abbott, Caroline Backlund
Wendy Buehr, Charles L. Mee, Jr.
COPY EDITOR
Mary Ann Pfeiffer
Assistants: Joan Rehe, Ruth H. Wolfe

ART DIRECTOR
Irwin Glusker
Associate Art Director: Elton Robinson

ADVISORY BOARD
Gilbert Highet, *Chairman*
Frederick Burkhardt   Oliver Jensen
Marshall B. Davidson   Jotham Johnson
Richard M. Ketchum   John Walker

EUROPEAN CONSULTING EDITOR
J. H. Plumb
Christ's College, Cambridge

EUROPEAN BUREAU
Gertrudis Feliu, *Chief*
11 rue du Bouloi, Paris

HORIZON is published every two months by American Heritage Publishing Co., Inc. Executive and editorial offices: 551 Fifth Ave., New York 17, N.Y. HORIZON welcomes contributions but can assume no responsibility for unsolicited material.

All correspondence about subscriptions should be addressed to: HORIZON Subscription Office, 379 West Center St., Marion, Ohio.

Single Copies: $4.50
Annual Subscriptions: $21.00 in the U.S. & Can. $22.00 elsewhere

An annual index is published every September, priced at $1. HORIZON is also indexed in the *Readers Guide to Periodical Literature.*

Title registered U.S. Patent Office
Second-class postage paid at New York, N.Y.

COVER: The pleasures of a day by the Seine were never more smilingly evoked than they are in this detail from Auguste Renoir's *Luncheon of the Boating Party* (1881). As any visitor to France knows, the river often flows beneath leaden skies or through grimy industrial districts; but in the mind's eye one sees it only in the timeless afternoon of French impressionism, where the season is most often summer. This is what the Seine owes to art. What art, literature, and philosophy owe to the Seine is the subject of an article beginning on page 52, written by Pierre Schneider and illustrated with more paintings and the photographs of Henri Cartier-Bresson. Renoir's *Boating Party* is in the Phillips Collection, Washington, D.C.

FRONTISPIECE: What might appear to be a Turkish Christmas tree is in fact a royal monogram from an official writ of Ibrahim I, Ottoman sultan from 1640 to 1648. The gold character at the base of the flowery illumination is Ibrahim's own signature. The script below it is the first line of the decree receiving a French consul at Constantinople in 1645. A passion for the ornamental was Ibrahim's only claim to distinction. He devoted his eight-year reign to collecting amber, perfumes, sable furs, and wives. His spree came to an end when the palace guard tired of his whims and strangled him.

In Lincoln Square did John D. III
　　　A stately palace of the arts decree,
Where architects and artists ran
　　　Through budgets measureless to man . . .
Culture doesn't come for free

NEW YORK'S MONUMENT

New York's Lincoln Center for the Performing Arts, which will declare itself open in September with a series of gala concerts in a new hall, is a unique attempt by the business community to play Medici on the American scene. When completed, probably in 1966–67, this vast enterprise will contain permanent homes for the New York Philharmonic, the Metropolitan Opera, and the Juilliard School of Music, as well as a repertory theatre, a 2,800-seat ballet theatre, a library, a museum, and a park with an outdoor bandstand. The total cost of the physical facilities will be at least $132 million and perhaps more than $140 million; and another $10 million will be placed in "a fund for education and artistic advancement," to give the Center itself some role beyond that of landlord. Contributions from federal, state, and local governments will make up $40 million of the total, assuming nothing goes wrong at the last minute at City Hall; the rest will have been raised (the Center is still more than $25 million short) from foundations, corporations, private individuals, and in one dramatic instance of foreign contribution, from the West German government.

No home for public spectacles has been built on so grand a scale since the fall of the Roman Empire. The enormous job of organizing, sustaining, and directing this effort has brought together, at meetings held at least every other week for the past seven years, a remarkable assemblage of New York corporate and financial executives—among them, Clarence Francis, former chairman of General Foods Corporation; Arthur A. Houghton, Jr., president of Steuben Glass; C. D. Jackson, vice president of Time Incorporated; Devereux Josephs, former chairman of New York Life Insurance Company; David Keiser, chairman of Cuban-American Sugar; and, as chairman and presiding mover and shaker of Lincoln Center, John D. Rockefeller III. Committees of advisers have proliferated below this golden Board, but the Grand Design comes almost exclusively from businessmen and their lawyers. Neither artists nor their traditional patrons, the hereditary landholders, have been represented at the moments of major decision; one looks in vain on the Board for the great New York *rentier* families, Astor, Goelet, Vanderbilt, Whitney, *et al.*, who once were the uncontested custodians of culture. There is a philosophy here—even if it does not have much to do with art—as well as a set of buildings.

Already, even before the doors open on the first of the buildings, Lincoln Center is a fascinating and important piece of American intellectual and social history. It is a lesson in how things get done, in who wants to get them done, and in where the power to get them done resides. It is a panorama of men and events moved by real estate and money, and by an idea of what constitutes public service. It is the story of a vision that began in high aspiration and has reached, even before the Center as such exists, a condition of aggravated dilemma. It is also a riddle that must be solved if New York's performing-art institutions are to flourish—or even maintain themselves—in their new surroundings.

The genesis of Lincoln Center can be traced to the late 1920's, when the elder John D. Rockefeller purchased his first leasehold in what is now Rockefeller Center, for the purpose of building a new opera house. Although this project vanished into the gathering gloom of the Depression, the men who had been associated with it remained liable to recurring seizures in which they saw façades, grand foyers, stage equipment, opening nights. Wallace K. Harrison, in 1930 a tall young architect who had begun to move in Rockefeller circles, kept in a place where he could easily get at them the preliminary sketches he had made. And the Rockefeller family, grandson Nelson in particular, saw in the land they had purchased in the West Fifties, just north of Rockefeller Center, an ideal place for an arts center, with opera house, concert hall, costume museum, and—the one structure actually built there—a museum of modern art.

In the political climate of the 1930's, however, this sort of complex could be built only with government co-operation. Fiorello LaGuardia, the closest New York City has ever come to having a musician as mayor, wanted to leave the city two legacies, an airfield and a music center, a home for the opera.

4

By MARTIN MAYER

TO THE MUSES

But these required the help of Robert Moses, then Parks Commissioner and already general panjandrum of public improvements. Though he is a lifelong Republican, Moses was at that time embittered by the rich and well-born who were trying to block his public-works projects. He took the position that opera was a dying art being kept alive for the diversion of socialites in the Diamond Horseshoe. "I think the Mayor buried the plan," Moses said recently, "because of some comments I made about the box holders."

But others kept the dream of a new opera house alive. Charles M. Spofford, diplomat and partner in the Wall Street law firm of Davis, Polk, Wardwell, Sunderland & Kiendl, had returned from World War II to become president of the Metropolitan Opera Association. Most of his board members wanted to stay where they were ("I love every inch of the gold curtain and want to be buried in it when I die"), but an engineering survey costing $25,000 had convinced them that the old 1883-vintage house on Thirty-ninth Street could not be brought up to modern standards of comfort and theatrical efficiency. Spofford and C. D. Jackson, of Time Incorporated, who had recently joined the board of the Metropolitan Opera, were authorized to scout around.

Before too long they became convinced that the real-estate market offered nothing of opera-house size. "When you began seeing where the plots of land were," Spofford says, "you knew the only way you could do it was Title I." Title I means the Federal Housing Authority slum-clearance program, and chairman of New York's Slum Clearance Committee was Robert Moses. As it happened, Moses was by this time deeply involved in city planning, along with everything else, and was no longer opposed to public help for a new Met. He offered them the plot just south of Washington Square where Washington Square Village now stands, but Spofford's audience and traffic surveys showed that it was unsuitable and anyhow, as one director said, "Nobody goes down there anymore."

Presently, in 1951, Moses as Slum Commissioner exercised the city's condemnation powers to purchase the land just west of Columbus Circle where Moses, as head of the Triborough Bridge Authority, later built an exposition hall called the Coliseum. It was the perfect site for a new opera house, but now came Moses's turn to back away from that idea, for reasons never fully explained. Moses says: "There was never any chance of an opera house at the Coliseum. Nobody really took it seriously." Jackson did. "I took it seriously enough to get a half a million dollars out of John D. Rockefeller, Jr., as a pledge to buy the land." But Moses was not prepared to go along, and let them know it, in March 1952, through the delicate device of a statement to the press.

Once the Coliseum plans were completed, Robert Moses turned his mind to the half-mile-long site north and west of it, centering on the spot where Broadway and Columbus Avenue cross to form Lincoln Square. Here, in this run-down, mainly Spanish-speaking neighborhood, he would bring about a masterpiece of slum clearance. Moses called Joseph Hartfield—senior partner of the Wall Street law firm of White & Case and a powerhouse on the Met's board—and offered him a site in the middle of the area that the city was planning to condemn and purchase. Max Abramovitz, a gentle and straightforward architect who is Wallace Harrison's partner, remembers that he, Spofford, and Hartfield rode the subway up to Sixty-sixth Street to look around: "Somebody said, 'What a hell of a neighborhood,'" Abramovitz recalls; "but here was all that land for virtually nothing."

With rising acrimony, the Met Board debated Moses's offer for more than a year. The site was in many ways unsatisfactory —an intersection that had a tendency to jam up even without an opera house on one corner, convenient to four bus lines but only one subway, surrounded by rather unappetizing structures. Then, in April, 1955, Moses got on the very top of the high horse he keeps for such emergencies and told Spofford this was the Met's "last chance"—it was Sixty-fourth Street or nothing, and the Met had better be ready with a million and a half dollars to buy the land by July first, or it would be nothing.

Spofford and Irving Olds, also a White & Case partner as well as chairman of U. S. Steel, set to work raising money. Wallace Harrison again began to make drawings for an opera house, and to sit in on meetings with members of the Met Board and Moses. "We were riding back from one of those meetings in a car," Spofford recalls, "and Wally Harrison said to me, 'You ought to get hold of Arthur Houghton, and bring the Philharmonic in.'"

It was from such high-level groupings that Lincoln Center was to emerge.

Of all the major symphony orchestras in the United States, the New York Philharmonic alone has played in a hall owned by a private, dividend-paying corporation. But the land Carnegie Hall occupied, just south of Central Park, was prime real estate, and in 1955, somewhat to its annoyance, the Board of the Philharmonic-Symphony Society was served with a three-year eviction notice and given an option to buy the building. Fortunately, the initial sale fell through—and Carnegie Hall was eventually saved from the knackers by a special act of the state legislature. For the Philharmonic had decided, quite early in the game, that it did not wish to buy Carnegie Hall. "The price asked," says Arthur Houghton of Steuben Glass, chairman of the Philharmonic, and occupant of Manhattan's last really enormous town house—"was quite substantial. The building was many years old, and quite frankly not architecturally distinguished. And acoustically it was *not* one of the great halls. We decided to look into the possibilities of building our own concert hall. We didn't have the resources to buy a prime corner site, but perhaps we could buy something in the center of a block, where we'd have to build only one façade. I asked Wally Harrison to come over. He built *this* building"—the reference is to the green Corning tower at Fifty-sixth Street and Fifth Avenue, where Houghton has his offices—"and he built our Corning Glass Center upstate. I asked Wally to make preliminary drawings and estimates. While I was talking, a peculiar expression passed over his face. He said the Met had just

approached him for a similar job, and perhaps I should get in touch with Chuck Spofford, see if we couldn't do something together—perhaps under one roof."

Spofford and Houghton dined together at the Knickerbocker Club, and quickly decided they needed a Rockefeller.

The problem was: *Which* Rockefeller? John D., Jr., was too old, and not well; Nelson already had political plans, and had been around the barn once too often with the Met, anyway; David was too busy working (quite successfully) to fill the giant shoes Winthrop Aldrich had left at the Chase Bank; Laurance was totally occupied building the American electronics industry and making embarrassingly large profits. Spofford's best bet, clearly, was John D. III, the eldest brother, a spare, modest, cautious man with bright blue eyes, who looks like photographs of his grandfather and who shares his grandfather's complete lack of interest in music. Spofford waited, and approached Rockefeller in Pennsylvania, at a conference on foreign relations in which they were both participants.

On his return to New York, Rockefeller called twenty or thirty people whom he knew to be interested in music, and asked them whether they thought the city needed a new opera house and a new concert hall. Receiving their encouragement, he agreed to head what came to be called the Exploratory Committee for a Musical Arts Center. "He is the kind of guy who does one major thing at a time," says C. D. Jackson. "He accepted *moral* responsibility for Lincoln Center."

Both the Met and the Philharmonic would have settled for new halls for themselves, but as Rockefeller consulted more people he saw the possibility of something much grander. Lincoln Kirstein, director of the New York City Ballet, was an old friend, and from Kirstein, Rockefeller knew that there was no adequate theatre for the dance in New York. Acquaintances interested in the theatre had complained to him about the fact that New York, unlike the great European capitals, had no repertory theatre. And by temperament and family tradition, Rockefeller felt that the reviving Center project should be linked to educational purposes as well. "We began," Houghton

6

recalls, "by talking about two buildings or one big building. Suddenly the thinking got explosive."

In early fall, 1955, the committee—which now included, among others, Kirstein, Olds, Harrison, and Devereux Josephs of the New York Life Insurance Company—began a schedule of luncheon meetings every other Monday, fair weather or foul, in all seasons. "We asked ourselves," Rockefeller remembers, "Do you stop with music? Or do you do all the performing arts? Or all the other arts as well? Then we asked, Do you bring education into the field? One of the factors was this need for bridging the gap between the performing groups and the teaching groups. After we had talked over all these matters for some time, I made a recommendation, a formal motion, at one of our meetings, that we do just the performing arts, and that education should be brought in. I remember Irving Olds said— it pleased me tremendously—'John, I thought we'd already all agreed on that.'"

Columbia University had recently announced its plans for an arts center. Rockefeller approached Columbia and also its neighbor on Riverside Drive, the renowned Juilliard School of Music. "Over the period of the conversations," Rockefeller recalls, "Juilliard got more and more enthusiastic about joining Lincoln Center, Columbia less and less." Eventually an agreement was reached with Juilliard whereby the school will institute, with money from Lincoln Center's special fund, a full-scale theatre program. "The other institutions," says William Schuman, the president of Juilliard who has since become President of Lincoln Center itself, "moved because they needed new buildings. We're moving because we believe in the idea."

Three institutions were now lined up, and Rockefeller was certain it would be only a matter of time before Kirstein's ballet company made a fourth. There remained the problem of the repertory theatre, later solved by the formation of a new institution under Robert Whitehead of Producers' Theatre, who received a $500,000 grant from the education fund to set up shop. The theatre, named after Mrs. Vivian Beaumont Allen, the May Company heiress who gave $3 million toward

its construction, will seat 1,100 in a wide, shallow auditorium. It has been designed to Whitehead's specifications ("nobody else will be able to use it") as the perfect setting for something that he says "must become an art theatre—in the sense that the Brecht Theatre became that, or the Théâtre National Populaire in Paris, at its best." Finally, to fill the other building the committee projected, the New York Public Library agreed to move its Music Division from the central building on Forty-second Street to a new home amid the sounds of Lincoln Center, in a museum of the performing arts.

By June, 1956, when the exploratory committee went out of business and Lincoln Center was incorporated, most of the major decisions had been made. There was going to be a Lincoln Center; the time had come to call in the technicians.

Oddly enough, nobody at any time seems to have questioned the central conception. "Everybody agreed," Spofford says, "that it was not only a good, it was a great idea." Nobody suggested that an arts center might be regarded as just a touch provincial for a cosmopolitan city—that in London, which has the world's busiest (though not the world's most interesting) concert, opera, and ballet season, the halls are so far apart it takes a good taxi ride to get from any one to any other; that even in Vienna, which has built a tourist trade on its residents' alleged musicality, the *Staatsoper* and the *Konzerthaus* are separated by several blocks of Ringstrasse.

The members of the exploratory committee found it only natural to assume that the whole of Lincoln Center would be bigger than the sum of its parts. They shared what Houghton calls "a feeling of exciting dedication," in an atmosphere far different from the dreary wrangling that characterizes the boards of the institutions themselves, and he found an analogy: "It's the kind of opportunity the Lenox and Astor Libraries and the Tilden Trust took when they joined together to build the New York Public Library." Raising money for all of the institutions together was clearly easier than raising it for any of them separately. To the Center's executive vice president, Ed-

7

The impetus for Lincoln Center came primarily from business and professional men who also take an interest in the arts. Among the most influential of them were (at left, left to right) Charles M. Spofford, diplomat and Wall Street lawyer; C. D. Jackson, vice president of Time Incorporated; and Arthur A. Houghton, Jr., president of Steuben Glass. After they brought the Metropolitan Opera together with the New York Philharmonic Orchestra, "the thinking got explosive."

gar B. Young, with years of experience at the Rockefeller Foundation, here was a chance to break the traditional patterns of philanthropy, the insistence on medicine and education, and lead both foundations and corporations to the idea of contributing to the performing arts. But there was never any guarantee that this excitement would persist. Moses, soured by the long delays, puts his finger on a sore spot when he says, "What is the relationship between Lincoln Center and its constituent elements? That's never been decided."

The problem has turned out to be a real one. It rose to the surface this past February with the announcement of seven nineteenth-century-style potpourri programs at benefit prices to launch Philharmonic Hall in September. Harold Schonberg, music critic of the New York *Times*, a supporter of Lincoln Center, expressed in print "the sinking feeling of a lover discovering that his beloved has false teeth." Rockefeller was disturbed. "Lincoln Center got jumped," he said, "for programs we didn't choose. One of the fundamentals is that the constituents are independent entities responsible for their own artistic programs and financing." Not until five years after the incorporation of Lincoln Center did the committee begin serious consideration of exactly *how* the whole was to be made larger than the sum of its parts.

Meanwhile, the show was on the road.

During the spring of 1956, members of the committee, including Rockefeller himself, traveled to Europe to visit concert halls, theatres, and opera houses, new and old, and to talk over problems with European managers, architects, and artists. In October of that year, theatre experts, acoustical consultants, and architects were assembled in New York for the first of several grand conferences. Among the architects were all those later assigned to buildings—Harrison (Metropolitan Opera; chairman of the group), his partner Abramovitz (Philharmonic Hall), Pietro Belluschi (Juilliard), the late Eero Saarinen (repertory theatre), Skidmore, Owings & Merrill (library-museum), and Philip Johnson (dance theatre, later called

New York State Theatre when the state put up the money)—plus Alvar Aalto of Finland, Sven Markelius of Sweden, Marcel Breuer, and Henry Shepley. They agreed on the proposition that the site was too small, and on very little else.

The architects' arguments were distressing to Rockefeller, who believes in consensus. "The major influence in this whole thing," says Harrison, "has been John's view of perfection." The committee had also felt a need to pick up a wholly outside opinion, from an organization that would not be involved in operating or building Lincoln Center. Money was appropriated for a full-scale "feasibility study," and the Philadelphia firm of Day & Zimmermann, consulting engineers, was assigned to the job.

With the Day & Zimmermann report, submitted on the last day of 1956, a shadow of innocence and naïveté falls across the prospects of Lincoln Center. Day & Zimmermann were basically builders of lofts, warehouses, and factories; and except in the case of the opera house, they had to operate virtually without instructions from their clients. They examined Carnegie Hall and existing theatres of approximately the seating capacity suggested for the other Lincoln Center halls, calculated the number of cubic feet occupied by each such building, and then applied a price of two dollars per cubic foot, which was about what it cost to build stripped-down movie theatres in the Philadelphia area in 1956. ("They forgot about air conditioning," says Abramovitz, "about the problem of isolating noises, about room for the people in back, offices, rehearsal rooms. . . .") They came up with a figure of $55 million for the land, the garage, the service plant, and all the buildings.

Day & Zimmermann thought the new concert hall could be built for $4 million (Abramovitz has brought it in at $15.4 million); the dance theatre for $5 million (estimates, in May, are $18.3); the education plant at $5.5 million (now $16.2 million); the repertory theatre and library-museum at $2.9 and $2.8 million (now $8.2 and $7 million, respectively). Only with the Met, which Day & Zimmermann estimated at $23.6 million (now $35.4 million), did the Philadelphians get as high

Of all the men closely concerned with the Center, only two have made the arts their full-time professional concern: Lincoln Kirstein (right), director of the N. Y. City Ballet; and William Schuman (far right), former president of the Juilliard School of Music. They hold opposing views of Lincoln Center's future. Schuman, now its president, sees "a dynamic and constructive force"; Kirstein, who has resigned from its Board, sees little more than "a real-estate scheme."

as half the now-projected costs. A $55 million estimate has risen to $132 million, and even the latter figure is still subject to possible upward revision, though only over Edgar Young's dead body.

The same astonishing blend of ignorance and optimism flavors the sections of the report that calculated operating expenses and revenues. The Met was assured, for example, that Lincoln Center could supply for a $263,000 annual rental the maintenance and clerical supplies and services which cost almost $700,000 at the old house. Projected rental charges on Philharmonic Hall were calculated on the assumption that the house would be used 470 times a year, though Carnegie had been rented only 310 times the season before. Proposing an operetta season in the new opera house to provide summer rentals, Day & Zimmermann suggested as a production that might fill the house for fourteen weeks the operetta *Rosalinda* by "J. Straus"—obviously unconscious of the fact that *Rosalinda* was merely an Anglicization of *Die Fledermaus,* which the Met had been playing throughout the previous season.

At a distance of five years, it is impossible to understand how the directors of Lincoln Center could have accepted the Day & Zimmermann report as their blueprint—but they did. The fund-raising target was set at $75 million, which Day & Zimmermann had recommended, to allow $19 million for contingencies and the education fund. And later, when the arguments began to arise about the size of the halls and their seating capacity, the Day & Zimmermann operating figures were always there as evidence that the Met and the Philharmonic could be virtually self-sustaining in Lincoln Center.

About half of Day & Zimmermann's amazing underestimate can be accounted for simply by the increased ambitiousness of the project. "It would have been disastrous," says Houghton, "to do anything less than what is magnificent." At every turn, until Edgar Young insulated them from the Board, the architects were able to appeal to the sponsors' pride in what they were building. Month after month the architects came to the building committee with improvements; and protesting they

would ne'er consent—they were businessmen, practical people, they had to keep an eye on what was financially feasible—the committee quickly consented.

"Imagine six architects, all working on a single site—six architects, compromising!" Thus Philip Johnson, architect (with Mies van der Rohe) of the Seagram Building, where he keeps his office. "We each imposed it on ourselves. We could have done a World's Fair, each man his own building, without regard for the others, but it wouldn't have been good for the project."

Nonetheless, beyond agreeing to hold the same cornice height, to use facings of light beige travertine from Italy, to keep first stories to the same height in all building, and to have austere exteriors planned around plain shafts of columns, the architects found it hard to make a unanimous recommendation to the building committee. Even when expanded, the site was awkward. Moses had set his little park and band shell immovably in the southwest corner, making an L-shaped pattern of buildings, which none of the architects wanted. Not long after the European architects departed, Harrison sold the committee on his original plan of a central plaza at Columbus Avenue, with the Met behind it and two other large buildings at either side. But there was still continuing debate over where each of the buildings should be spotted.

Meanwhile, 1957 disappeared into history and 1958 wore on with victorious lawsuits, fund-raising, purchases of land, careful relocation of tenants, and—on July 21—the first demolitions on the site. The Philharmonic was supposed to be ready first, but it could not be built on the southwest corner, because a large warehouse still stood there, immune to proceedings under the slum-clearance laws and demanding a separately negotiated purchase. (The warehouse was owned by Joseph P. Kennedy, who exacted a price more than double the assessed valuation.) Presently, the northeast corner of the site was clear of buildings, and it became obvious that this location, always plausible, was where the Philharmonic had to be.

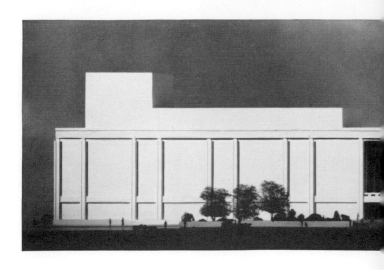

When and if the dream is finally realized, it should look something like the model at right. The buildings (left to right) are the New York State Theatre, the Metropolitan Opera, Philharmonic Hall, and the Juilliard School and Chamber Music and Recital Hall. (Concealed by Philharmonic Hall are the Vivian Beaumont Repertory Theatre and the Library-Museum.) Fund-raising for Lincoln Center continues among corporations, foundations, and even foreign governments. As summer neared, some $28,000,000 were still being sought.

For the architects, the Lincoln Center buildings have been a staggering job. Harrison has given the bulk of his time to the opera house for more than six years, and the drawings are still far from finished. Moses says, "I used to drop by Harrison's place at West Hills, after a party, at one in the morning, on Saturdays, and I'd find Wally and Wong, who ran the drafting room, down the root cellar, making drawings and looking at models."

The Philharmonic's requirements, as Abramovitz recalls them, were simple in the extreme: "They wanted a hall at least as good as Carnegie, and three thousand seats." Then Abramovitz's acoustical consultants—Leo Beranek of the M.I.T.-based firm of Bolt, Beranek & Newman, aided by Hope Bagenal of England—told him the two desires were incompatible. Given modern fire laws and modern comfort, they were not prepared to recommend anything larger than a hall of 750,000 cubic feet, with 2,400 seats. Several years of argument back and forth (every time Beranek disapproved an idea, Abramovitz would call Bagenal, only to hear the old man say softly, "Oh, Max, don't do it; I've done it, and it was awful") pushed Beranek to 850,000 cubic feet and 2,600 bodies, but no more. "I would push him until I saw he was afraid," Abramovitz remembers. "I never push a consultant beyond the point of fear."

Everything about Philharmonic Hall had to be cleared with Beranek; and the other architects, watching the complications Beranek created in Abramovitz's designs, vowed they would have none of it. Acoustics is not an exact science; different consultants go different ways. Johnson, the free spirit of the group, went to Denmark and got an acoustical consultant who would approve the "baroque theatre" he and George Balanchine wanted for the dance, with balconies disguised as antique boxes one row deep all along the walls. Harrison has worked with Beranek, and with Danes, and with Germans, and with a man at Bell Labs who has a machine that, in theory, can simulate the sound of a hall. But there is no escaping the acoustics engineer; the first question must be how the music will sound.

The problems the acoustical consultants set the architects were as nothing compared to the problems they set for the directors of Lincoln Center. The two original constituents, the Philharmonic and the Met, both required considerably larger seating capacity if they were ever to hope for escape from large annual deficits—the Met in all its planning had counted on 4,500 seats, at least 700 more than it will get. In the end, however, despite what Spofford describes as "quite a hue and cry within the Boards," Lincoln Center had to be governed by Rockefeller's view of perfection.

There was no escaping the consequence. The "orientation to quality," as Edgar Young calls it, would leave the performing institutions with leases that must cover maintenance costs on luxurious buildings, and with seating capacities inadequate to meet the bills—unless seats could be sold at substantially higher prices, which nobody wanted to see. Assuming that the New York City Center opera and ballet companies wind up in the New York State Theatre, which both John D. Rockefeller III and Moses still insist must happen, the total subsidy required to operate the four performing institutions, even at good attendance, would run around $3 million a year. Where was it going to come from? At this point the leaders of Lincoln Center put their trust in Business; It would provide. "These men of affairs," says William Schuman admiringly, "are basically men of faith."

In May, 1959, Lincoln Kirstein resigned as a director. Lincoln Center, he said, is nothing more than "a question of clean facilities. I was led to believe it was a heroic, idealistic effort, and it turns out to be a real-estate scheme. I'm not interested in real estate."

Kirstein believes Lincoln Center has priced out of his reach the theatre that was being built for his New York City Ballet; and he finds it scandalous that a committee willing to approve expensive enlargements of buildings should send him begging to the state and the city for the $400,000 annual subsidy he would need to operate in the New York State Theatre. "There's no generosity anywhere here," he says, "no real patronage."

Kirstein wonders what Lincoln Center expects to do with the New York State Theatre, which will have an interior cubic volume almost exactly as large as that of the old Metropolitan Opera, and will thus be much too big for the kind of attraction (Old Vic, D'Oyly Carte, Viennese operetta, etc.) Reginald Allen, the Center's executive director, has talked about putting on that stage. (Philip Johnson, rather cynically, agrees: "The whole trick in designing this theatre," he says, "is to make it look full when it's two-thirds empty. I don't have the vaguest notion what they can use it for; the last theatre this size in New York had to be torn down because it was always vacant.") Kirstein feels he has been asked to lead the City Center to the New York State Theatre on terms that would force the opera and ballet companies to play for a sellout every night. "I'm not interested in normal operations," Kirstein says. "I'm interested in surplus. The distinction of an institution lies in how wasteful it is, wasteful in ideas, talent, art." Kirstein foresees a Lincoln Center in which the constituents, struggling annually against horrifying deficits, dare not risk a new opera, a new play, a new idea.

Of all the people who have been involved in the direction of Lincoln Center, two alone have given their whole lives to the arts: one is Kirstein and the other is William Schuman, the composer who became president of the Center in 1962. Schuman's view of the Center is that it will be "a dynamic and constructive force in the arts." Obviously, these two men hear different drummers.

Cut away from their old roots, Schuman expects the constituents will have to develop new habits. "Lincoln Center will sponsor projects to strengthen the constituents and bring other activities into the Center. We will educate the public to new works, whether they prove provocative or provoking. We will sponsor the first major American festival of international scope, music, opera, choral, dance, theatre, and film. There will be a Lincoln Center Teachers' Institute. We will bring to the Center every summer four to six hundred teachers, who will come a minimum of two summers, perhaps three, the

teachers of speech to act under a Harold Clurman, the pianists to study with a Rosina Lhevinne or a Beveridge Webster, the teachers of dance to do ballets under a Balanchine, a Tudor, a Limon. The core of Lincoln Center will be the fund for education and artistic advancement, which will require continuous fund-raising, to establish a situation where we don't have a hand-to-mouth existence. But the money will be there."

Maybe so. The odds against Schuman and the Center are high, but they are not prohibitive. The shining existence of this monument to a belief in Culture may indeed draw new foundation and corporate contributors to the performing arts, on a continuing basis. Failing adequate private support, Lincoln Center will be able to make a stronger case than any single institution for city or state or Federal subsidy—in fact, Federal subsidy has been much in the minds and the mouths of the directors of Lincoln Center for the past eighteen months. ("What was once a dirty word," C. D. Jackson says, "is now a thoughtful proposition.") Finally, Lincoln Center has something going for it which cannot be weighted in any known balance—the excitement of new halls. Even in an age when rockets aim for the moon, there is for anyone at all sensitive to these matters a great thrill, a leap of the heart, at the first sight of the mastery of space represented by a large concert hall or opera house. Perhaps this thrill will act upon creative artists, performing artists, and audiences with such power that all merely practical considerations will triumphantly be swept aside.

The future is, as always, in the hands of the artists. It may be twenty or thirty years from now before New York will know whether or not to thank the powerful, dedicated, oddly impractical businessmen who have created for their city this monument to their respectful, distant, and refreshingly innocent confidence in Art. Lincoln Center, as the businessmen planned it, has no built-in aesthetic purpose. The artists may find one.

Martin Mayer, whose latest book is The Schools, *wrote "Ford Moves in on the Arts" in the January, 1962, issue of* HORIZON.

NATIONALMUSEUM, STOCKHOLM

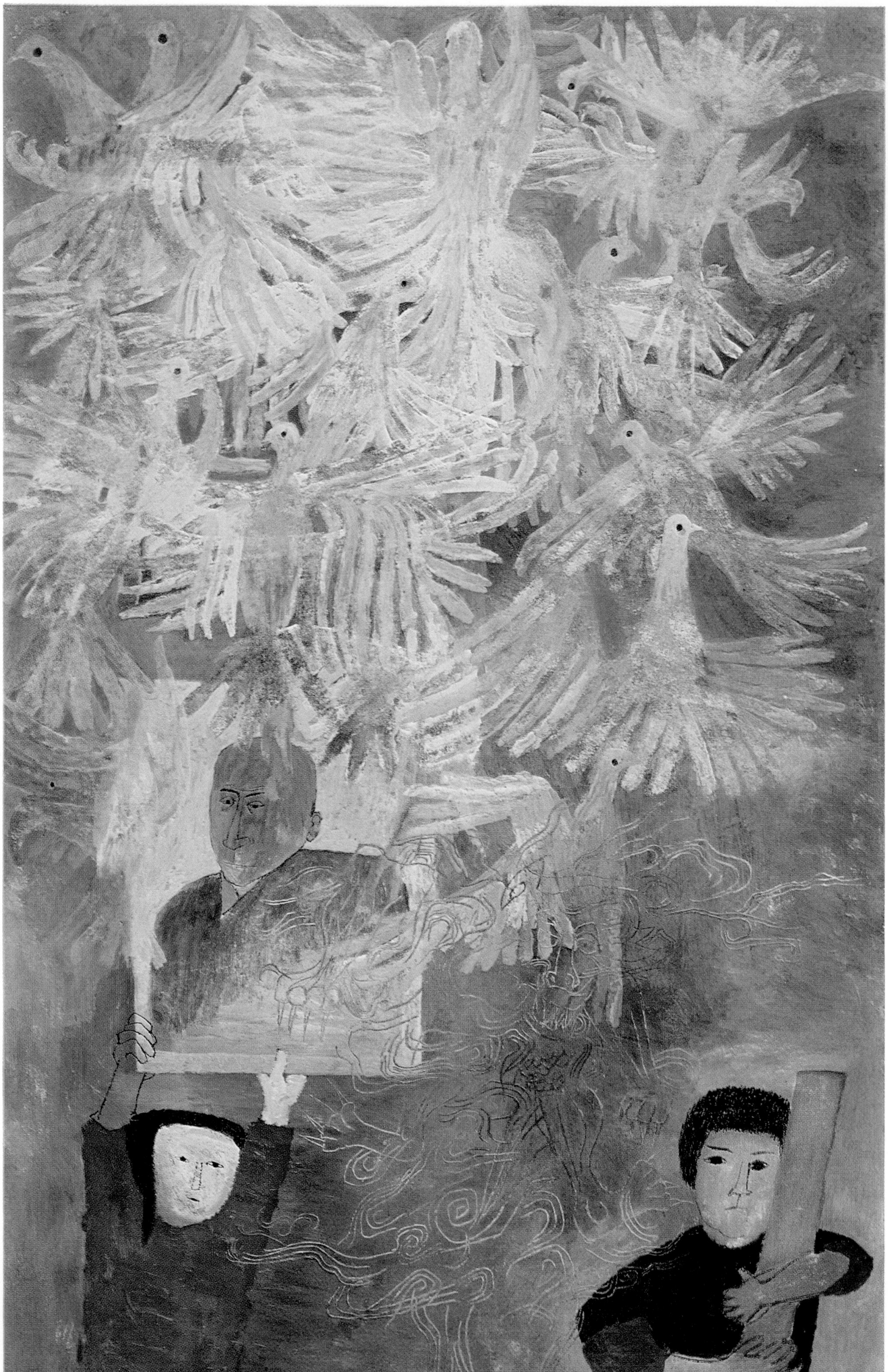

Consigned to oblivion when the abstract expressionists carried the day, many of those artists who never joined up now find themselves being recalled from exile

Art Against the Grain

Ben Shahn *has always been communicative, both in and about his art. "Compassion for suffering," he once said, "has been the constant intention of my work since I first picked up a paintbrush"; and the evidence is in every picture he ever painted. Born in Lithuania sixty-four years ago, he grew up in New York City and supported himself, while still in his teens, as a lithographer's assistant. Since then he has designed and illustrated books, done murals for public buildings and, during the Depression, made evocative photographs for the Farm Security Administration. But his concern for a comprehensible truth comes out most clearly in his paintings, beginning in the thirties with a famous series on the Sacco-Vanzetti trial. A* Score of White Pigeons *(opposite) is from a new series he exhibited last fall under the title of "The Saga of the Lucky Dragon," named for the Japanese fishing boat that unluckily sailed into the fall-out of the American H-bomb test at Bikini in 1954. Holding aloft a portrait of one of the dead fishermen, two Japanese children release the white doves of peace—while beneath the triumphant beat of the birds' wings one sees the fire-dragon, Shahn's symbol of atomic death.*

To look casually at the art scene in America is to be convinced instantly that there is a single, universally accepted way of painting, a way which has produced, without exception, all the artists of consequence who now enjoy fame in this country, and from which no artist of consequence departs very far. It is broad enough to include the lush paint drippings of its single best-known practitioner, the late Jackson Pollock, the austere yet gigantic strokes of black on vast white of Franz Kline, and the no less enormous but softer and flatter fields of two or three colors by Mark Rothko, these being but three leaders of a multitude of painters who follow The Way.

Easier to name than to describe, it has been called any number of things: psychologically, abstract expressionism; therapeutically, "action" painting; geographically, the New York School; and generally, the New American Painting. For about a dozen years the painting identified by these names has seemed to dominate the art scene. It has occupied the most space in national exhibitions. It has taken over most of the American representation in international exhibitions. It has annexed most of the color reproductions and text space in art magazines. It has called into existence an industrious set of writers able to explain not only why it is so excellent but why most painting of the past was really only a precursor of today's ruling style. It has attracted collectors, individual and institutional, able and willing to keep up with the moon-flight rise of the price tags. And, dictating taste, it has become an art "academy" as narrow and as rigid as any that ever held sway: as authoritarian as the Royal Academy in nineteenth-century England, as the Salon of Napoleon III, as the National Academy in this country around the turn of the century.

But contrary to appearances, a large number of American painters are not totally bemused by the patterns paint makes when it

By FRANK GETLEIN

COLLECTION ROY R. NEUBERGER

Even though Willem de Kooning became— and remains—a faithful abstract expressionist, a portrait of sorts was lurking in the brushwork of his Marilyn Monroe *(1954).*

is flung, squirted, dripped, dropped, rolled, roiled, boiled, and burned. Contrary to appearances, appearances themselves are still the concern of some American painters—the way things look in different weathers and different moods, the way things are, and the way things seem to be. Many American painters work steadily and successfully against the grain of what has become, in effect, our official art. They include older artists who never caught the trick of recklessly flinging their emotions onto canvas and younger artists who, having learned it as the first and last rule of art, grew bored with it. Until quite recently the power of the ruling school has been so great and so universal that these nonconformists have been thrust into a kind of limbo as far as publicity is concerned. Not appearing in major museum exhibitions, in color spreads and review columns of major art magazines, or in illustrated art books on contemporary American painting, these individualistic painters have, in the view of many custodians of our "official" art, simply ceased to exist.

Not so. They exist—and to such purpose that they seem now on the point of breaking out of oblivion. Over the past three or four years they have begun to recover lost ground in major exhibitions, in the acquisition programs of leading museums, and in the editorial columns of at least some art publications.

While the dominant mode and all its variants cannot be satisfactorily described, their common traits can be noted, and the commonest is this: that none of these paintings bears the faintest resemblance to anything but paint, just plain paint, distributed on a surface in such a way that the process of distribution remains evident. Exceptions can be made, most notably in the case of Willem de Kooning, who once did a portrait of Marilyn Monroe (at left) and from whose latest paintings the figure of a woman sometimes seems to be emerging. But the exception is permitted, one suspects, only because the broad caricature strokes of the portrait enabled partisans of our official art to imagine that Miss Monroe had emerged by accident from the normal frenzy of De Kooning's paint—rather like the *Complete Works of Charles Dickens* coming from the typewriters of those fabled apes.

The rule remains: if you can tell what it is, it isn't any good, should not be exhibited, and should preferably not be reproduced or discussed. In a period when art is uniquely dependent upon publicity, this is the same as saying: if you can tell what it is, it doesn't exist at all. It's an odd rule, when you think of it, and all the odder when you think that most of the institutions that enforce it either came into existence or took on their present character in protest against the enforcing of rules in art.

The Museum of Modern Art in New York, for example, is probably the most important of the institutions that annually say what is valid art. Historically, such a role should be totally repugnant to that Museum's spirit: its idea, when it was founded, was to make available art that was being overlooked or suppressed by more academic institutions.

14

Rico Lebrun has used simplified images, as in his mural of Genesis *at Pomona College, California, but his work has always been rooted in the classic tradition of painting.*

Success in this effort led to the establishment of the Modern as a kind of reluctant tastemaker, with what often looked like a policy of a new frontier for every new winter season. The trouble with tastemaking, however reluctant, is that once a taste is made, there is a substantial investment in it—an investment of reputation, of intellectual interest, and of cash. The growth of abstract expressionism as the established mode was paralleled by the growth of tailfins and headlights on American automobiles: there was just too much money tied up in them, from the dies to the advertising mystique of the swollen fender, to risk rocking the boat.

In politics, the revolutionary radical of today regularly becomes the totalitarian Grand Inquisitor of tomorrow. This is no less true in art: institutional and administrative dedication to freedom has produced a conformity more complete than any in ages.

Yet opposition persists. Painters rebelled against the French Salon, the Royal Academy, and the National Academy when those institutions dictated taste. Now they rebel against the new academy of abstract expressionism. These "underground" painters are concerned in their work with something other than the act of painting itself. Engrossed in it as an art and as a craft, they nevertheless feel compelled to look at the world and to paint what they see.

Broadly speaking, painters like Ben Shahn and Jack Levine paint aspects of man's social tragedy in pictures of men and women so conceived as to reveal that tragedy (see pages 12 and 16). Andrew Wyeth paints in gripping clarity spare, haunted landscapes or isolated moments in the lives of rural people. Aaron Bohrod and Peter Blume both plumb the meaning of life through selected symbols painted in very sharp focus. Focus is softened, even misted over, in Loren MacIver's poetic views of the city and its corners, suggesting the unity of separate things and the unity of all with the viewer (see page 21). Georgia O'Keeffe can reveal the universe or measure death and infinity with, say, a bleached pelvic bone against a shining sky. More conventionally but no less effectively, Alexander Brook can find the desolation in an interior or a figure (see page 17) and Walter Stuempfig the romantic stillness in an industrial landscape. Milton Avery simplifies color and form in landscapes and uses new versions of the human figure to convey the distance or the closeness between human souls (see page 20). Abraham Rattner and Rico Lebrun painfully distort the figure to reveal fresh anguish in such ancient subjects as the deposition of Christ and such modern ones as Buchenwald and Dachau. Edward Hopper and Raphael Soyer use a quiet insistence on light and form to show the loneliness and drudgery of the city.

They seek, each in his own way, to paint as well as they can in order to reveal what they see, each in his own way, of the human condition. If they now find themselves in an unaccustomed role, it is not from choice. They did not set themselves against the prevailing taste; rather, the taste for abstract expressionism moved in on an art world they already occupied, dispossessed them, and

TEXT CONTINUED ON PAGE 18

15

Jack Levine *grew up in the seamy precincts of South Boston, where he became at an early age both a moralist and a traditionalist. Today, at forty-seven, he is one of the most outspoken of American artists, both on questions of public justice and on the need for remaining faithful to the great tradition in art, even while bringing it up to date. For the high-flying abstract expressionists, his mildest term is "space cadets." Of himself he has said: "I am equipped to punish." And even though not all of his work involves social criticism, many of his most brilliant paintings have been punishing portraits of the cruel and the corrupt; for example,* The Spanish Prison *(1961). The guard's hat shadows his eyes like an executioner's mask, and balances the obliterating gag across the prisoner's mouth. The few vivid spots of color are all local references to the soldier's decorations and insignia, yet they float on the surface of the painting to convey the aura of power; the dry, dirty white of the prisoner's flesh and shirt reflects accurate observation, yet it is also the color of the plastered wall against which a man is stood up to be shot.*

Alexander Brook *is one of the few contemporary American artists who can still seat themselves before a canvas and a model (models went out of style when cubism came in half a century ago) and bring the two together with meaning for himself and his audience. Thus* Malagueña *(1958) is much more than the merely sumptuous nude it might have been: the somber color, the perfect balance of the composition, the scarf isolating and emphasizing the face—all serve to check the viewer's sensuality; the object of desire has become an object of contemplation. Now sixty-four, Brook first achieved recognition in his and the century's mid-twenties with a one-man show at the Whitney Studio Club, one of the forerunners of the Whitney Museum of American Art. He has always demanded pleasure of his painting, and his sensuous handling of the paint itself shows that he really enjoys it. Throughout his career he has been able to live well from portraits, never lacking for commissions despite—or perhaps because of—his customary warning to a sitter: "If I don't like it, I'll destroy it; if you don't like it, I'll keep it and sell it as a painting."*

Walter Stuemphig's The Waterworks *(1947) characteristically transforms a drab urban scene into a romantic Italianate landscape.*

Cyrano (1962) is typical of Aaron Bohrod's sharp-focus, fool-the-eye still lifes that use associations to evoke a person or mood.

TEXT CONTINUED FROM PAGE 15

eventually imposed the rigid conformity we now see on all sides.

A great deal of the art history of the past two centuries is the history of officially derided art, which gradually, in the lifetime of its creators or after, has been allowed to come to the surface. By the same token much of the officially approved art of other days is now seen to be pure bombast, falsification, and pandering. The French Revolution and the Napoleonic Wars, for example, included an immense amount of human suffering. But the Salon-approved artist of these events, Jacques Louis David, shows us nothing of this; he shows us chiefly *la gloire*.

A similar kind of falsification went on in the scenes of happy peasants and workers painted in Europe and widely popular in America before and after the turn of the century. Charles Dickens, Karl Marx, and Frank Norris have shown us certain prominent aspects of the past century's industrial Coketown. The place didn't exist at all in the official art of the time. There, the lower classes were well fed, deferential to their betters, amusing in their ignorance, happy, and above all clean.

This tendency has been carried to its logical conclusion today: reality as a whole has ceased to exist, its place being taken by the artist's sensitivity to his materials and methods.

The role that Salon art played in the past in pandering to suppressed desires is also painfully obvious. All those pneumatic nudes of Bouguereau and Cabanel may have been labeled *Hope* or *The Christian Martyrs* or *The Values of a Classical Education*, but they were first of all compact and rounded young ladies without

18

Abraham Rattner's painting is becoming increasingly abstract, but in his Job No. 2 *(1958) the imploring figure is still legible.*

any clothes on. More than that. Very often they were completely at the mercy of some dominant male or males: the slave dealer, the slave purchaser, the decadent Roman Emperor, the lion in the arena, and—in all these guises—the Salon visitor or picture buyer himself.

No less does today's predominant style lend itself to a reading in terms of the otherwise unexpressed psychic goals of its admirers and purchasers. They are generally the somewhat more civilized successors to the Salon's patrons—brokers and bankers, light manufacturers, network officials, and agency vice-presidents. Part of the fascination they find in abstract expressionism may have been anticipated by the financier and collector Solomon Guggenheim, explaining what he liked about Kandinsky. "All day long," he is reported to have said, "I add up columns of figures and make everything balance. I come home. I sit down. I look at a Kandinsky, and it's wonderful. It doesn't mean a thing, and there's nothing to understand."

A note common to all the various manifestations of our own official art is violent disorder, whether it is that of spilled paint or that of junked automobiles. If it is at all valid to read meaning into tastes and fashions, it is somewhat frightening to think of our captains of finance, of mass communication, and of advertising sitting in their rectangularly austere offices and contemplating their hidden desires in images of everything gone smash.

Oddly enough, the establishment of our present native Salon came about in part through the violent propaganda efforts of an underground artist who began demanding thirty years ago that American art institutions pay attention to American art and succeeded beyond his wildest dreams. The artist was Thomas Hart Benton. When he began proselytizing for American art, there were many in the art world who thought there was no such thing, never had been, never would be. If you had really big money, you went in for Italian Renaissance painting; if you wanted to be up to date, you went in for French. All through the thirties and well into the forties Benton kept up his shrill, insistent attack, and eventually he was heard. Like Moses at the edge of Canaan, Benton himself never quite made it into the Promised Land. It was left to Benton's star pupil, Jackson Pollock, to cross the Jordan, establish the kingdom, and become the center of a new official art that, as a matter of course, exiled Benton to the walls of Presidential libraries in Independence, Missouri, and power stations at Niagara Falls.

Even odder is the fact that the new American art achieved its status, in part at least, because so many museum men were poignantly aware of the sins of their predecessors. According to the record, those tastemakers of former times had dismally failed because they looked at canvases by Courbet, Renoir, Manet, Van Gogh, Gauguin, Cézanne, Matisse, and Picasso, and saw what they took to be the work of lunatics or simply incompetents. This mistake, it was institutionally resolved, must not happen again. The

TEXT CONTINUED ON PAGE 24

Milton Avery—*born in New York State, reared in Connecticut, and a frequent summer resident of Cape Cod and Vermont—has a Yankee frugality in both his forms and his pigments. The forms (of women, woods, beaches, meadows, animals, and household objects) are so simplified as to be contained within what often seems one unbroken line, yet the course of the line is so true that it suggests volume and weight as well as outline. He paints with a minimum of colors, getting a bigger bang, visually, out of a lemon, a lime, a blue, and a gray than many painters do from the whole juicy spectrum. His work has often been compared with Matisse's—the flat forms, the clear colors. The resemblance is visible here in* Interlude *(1960), but the feeling of the painting is closer to Bonnard. Although faceless, the two women are obviously known and loved, and their presence saturates the whole painting, as the yellow of the nearer one's dress is diffused through the air. Now sixty-nine, Avery has survived through the years by his own total dedication to his art and by the equally intense dedication of his wife, the widely known illustrator Sally Michel.*

Loren MacIver *has never strayed for long, in art or in life, from New York City: she was born there in 1909, went to its public schools, studied at its Art Students League, married a poet she had met in high school (Lloyd Frankenberg), and has lived in Greenwich Village ever since, except for summers on Cape Cod and occasional trips to Europe. This personal history is reflected in her work. If she has sometimes painted an Irish meadow or Venice from the lagoon, and found the expected poetry in them, she has spent as much or more time revealing the unexpected poetry of New York: oil slicks on a wet sidewalk, snow against the grid of a skylight, the secrets of some private urban corner. Often the parts are rearranged, often the light shimmers through a mist that only the unseeing would think of as smog. In* Manhattan *(1959) she grasps the whole city scheme of things. The swarm of earth-bound pedestrians and autos, at the lower left, turns like a flight of birds into soaring citizens guarded by helicopters, and moves lightly toward the blue sky that shines everywhere between the tall towers of Loren MacIver's New York.*

Robert Broderson *is one of the young painters who have been developing a distinctive style outside the prevailing mode of abstract expressionism, even though it has influenced his way of applying paint to canvas. He began painting about fifteen years ago, when he was twenty-seven or twenty-eight—rather late in life by today's precocious standards. But, as he says, "What difference does it make? If you're alive and looking up, you've been soaking up material all that time." His material comes from reading and from memories of his childhood in Connecticut, which he recalls as rather lonely and filled with daydreams. He says his painting is literary to the extent that he likes to tell stories, but they are certainly not literal ones. Many of his canvases, in fact, have the unreal reality of dreams: a typical example is* Memory of Childhood *(1961), with its stark but effective color, its brooding boys, its enigmatic birds and beasts, and its strangely lighted sky. Broderson is currently an assistant professor of art at Duke University in Durham, North Carolina, and recipient of a $2000 award from the National Institute of Arts and Letters.*

Ben Kamihira *was born in Yakima, Washington, in 1925, but studied at the Pennsylvania Academy of Fine Arts and now teaches there—thus fitting into a Philadelphia tradition of realism that goes back to the Peales and the founding of the Republic. Not that his work has much in common with those confident times: it is somber and sometimes rather frightening. His images reveal, in the abnormally clear light of hallucination, a chill perception of the human condition. The emphasis is on the inextricably mixed relations of growth and decay. Miyo (1961) frames the young-old girl of its title with three plants which, though different species, look like variations of one another and, all three, like variations of Miyo herself. The glossy leaves are shiny with life, yet seem already overripe. The painter continues this loading of symbolic values into ordinary objects all the way through: the silver tray, round and blank and dull, echoes this troubling adolescence as do the plants; so does the ungainly sideboard, its curved legs as awkward as Miyo's; while the crumpled letters mock the girlish white slip.*

Colleen Browning's Comtesse Lucine and Sabine Savelli *(1961) was painted in Corsica, as were some evocative landscapes.*

TEXT CONTINUED FROM PAGE 19

timely arrival of abstract expressionism gave them a marvelous chance to show their sincerity. They seized it, and have been resolutely showing their open-mindedness ever since.

So thoroughly, in fact, has this atonement been made that the rebellious avant-garde suddenly finds itself with nothing to rebel against and nothing to be in advance of. The drive to be original, to create an entirely different look, has failed, as it had to, for the simple reason that while there are certainly a great many ways to put paint on canvas, the number is finite and the end has been reached. This is easily recognized by the visitor to any new-talent show. But it has also been recognized by the avant-garde itself. Proclaiming that Pollock killed painting, the younger artists have gone on to other things, such as exhibiting the wreckage of automobiles or empty beer cans cast in bronze. More significant still, the guard has advanced into "happenings" and "environments," neither of which can be contained in any great number in a museum. Roughly, an "environment" is a free-form interior, painted, carpentered, or assembled, while a "happening" is more or less the same thing with something going on inside it—a sequence of events arranged and acted not by playwrights or actors but by people who once would have been painters.

Meanwhile, back at the art museum, there were the walls, there was the thirst for the new, there was the accepted obligation to recognize the unrecognized. The result, of course, has been the readmittance to respectability of the only kind of painting kept out by the new academy of abstract expressionism: realistic, representational, figurative, or by whatever name, the painting of Americans interested in making pictures relating to the objective world about them.

What has been called the "return" to figurative painting began showing up in big exhibitions as early as four years ago. By last season this "return" began to hold its own in major exhibitions, and the summer of 1962 has seen the Museum of Modern Art itself exhibiting recent figure paintings. The word "return" is deceptive. Most of the painters illustrated in these pages haven't returned to the figurative: they never left.

They have, however, been joined in growing numbers by younger artists unable or unwilling to master the self-indulgences of abstract expressionism—one how-to-do-it book on the subject says "when painting begins you must be prepared to let yourself go"—and suddenly anxious to get to work at the ancient task of art, the double task of seeing the world and creating a world.

Again, there is neither organization, common program, nor shared look among the younger painters of man's world. The closest approach to a group has been the three West Coast painters, Richard Diebenkorn, Elmer Bischoff, and David Park,* all of whom discovered that the broad brush strokes of abstract expressionism can be effective for new visions of the old world, that of sunlight and shadow and people caught between them.

But most of these artists are loners, pursuing their separate

* See "Figures to the Fore" by Eleanor C. Munro, in HORIZON for July, 1960.

*David Aronson's archaic, legendary figures
—this is* Conjuror I *(1960)—come from
Jewish mythology or the Old Testament.*

ends. Ben Kamihira paints as if there had never been a predominant, anti-figurative art (see page 23). Robert Broderson gets compression and power from some of the techniques of that art (see page 22). David Aronson, in Boston, paints crude but moving figures of Biblical personages. Colleen Browning, an Irish girl in New York, paints smooth but no less moving figures of street children in Spanish Harlem or Corsica. William Congdon, long a painter of semiabstract landscapes, last winter showed that abstract expressionist technique could be moved over intact into the painting of devotional images.

The means vary. The aim is constant, the heart of man to be reached through images he can see and know. Needless to say, the aim is not always achieved by these painters of the human figure or of the world. But in many cases it is. And it is pleasant that our art, once more, is permitted to be human.

Frank Getlein is the art critic of both The New Republic *and the* Washington Star. HORIZON *published excerpts from his most recent book,* A Modern Demonology, *in July and September, 1961.*

*William Congdon is now treating powerful
religious themes with a slashing, expressionist technique, as in* Christ Derided *(1961).*

25

NEW LIFE AMONG THE RUINS

Moses, legend says,

once struck open Petra's

deep crevasse.

Now many far-flung

ancient sites are

responding to fresh batons

While archaeologists are exhuming and rehabilitating ever more sites along the eastern Mediterranean that testify to the splendor of Rome's empire at its zenith, today in many instances they are followed by entrepreneurs and artists who use these ancient theatres, temples, and arenas for living performances and festivals, thus in a sense completing their revival. From Roman Athens to such remote reminders of past glories as the "lost" city of Petra in the Jordanian desert, Herod's Caesarea on the coast of Israel, and the fabled temples of Baalbek in Lebanon (see following pages) the spade is now being succeeded by klieg light, dancing platform, and music stand.

The latest as well as the remotest to be restored to light and life is Petra, Jordan's "rose-red city, half as old as Time," where audiences this summer will fill its amphitheatre (see overleaf) for the first time in nearly seventeen centuries. A thieves' stronghold in 500 B.C., later the secluded capital of the nomadic Nabateans, Petra was conquered by Trajan in A.D. 106 to become one of the Roman Empire's most influential outposts. Its appeal to thieves, nomads, and Romans alike was its impregnability and its proximity to caravan trade routes: men and treasure could enter it only through the easily defended Siq, the narrow defile shown opposite, whose sheer walls rise 300 feet high. According to legend, this crevasse opened when it was struck by the rod of Moses. Petra's appeal to visitors today, though, comes from monumental edifices like the well-preserved Treasury at left, sculpted from the living sandstone.

PHOTO APPIA

Aunique, handcarved cliff city in rugged and forbidding country just under a hundred miles south of Jerusalem, Petra was forgotten by the Western world when the trade routes passing it died out early in the Christian era and was rediscovered only in 1812 by the Swiss archaeologist Johann Burckhardt.

Last year Dr. Philip C. Hammond of Princeton Theological Seminary led an expedition to Petra and, with the aid of the Jordanian government, restored its Roman amphitheatre (left, before the work began) in time to celebrate the 150th anniversary of Burckhardt's finds. Among Dr. Hammond's discoveries at the site is the fragment of stone above, incised with part of the Roman word "theatre." Below is the stage itself, photographed in process of restoration. The celebration festival this September will include a concert by the Arab Legion drum and bagpipe corps and an exhibition of horse handling and racing by expert Bedouin riders.

PHILIP C. HAMMOND

DON HUNSTEIN—COLUMBIA RECORDS

lose under the southwestern slope of the Acropolis, after the Romans conquered Athens early in the Christian era, they built a vast amphitheatre of their own. In 1959 it formed the setting for a performance (seen at upper left) of the New York Philharmonic under Leonard Bernstein. The seven-year-old Athens festival this season will present the Berlin Philharmonic and the National Theatre of Greece. Among new festivals at old sites is the one now in its second year at Caesarea, Israel, a Mediterranean port built by Herod the Great in 10 B.C. and conquered by the Romans soon thereafter. Though much of the city's ruins are under sand and water, archaeologists have revived the theatre; there (lower left) Isaac Stern, Eugene Istomin, and Leonard Rose performed Beethoven's "Ghost" trio at last year's festival. This summer the Caesarea program will include the "Piraikon," a Greek theatre group.

Baalbek, the ancient Heliopolis deep in the Bekaa Valley of present-day Lebanon, once lured Pompey, Antony, and Nero in turn to consult the renowned oracles at its temples of Bacchus and Jupiter, then considered among the most imposing in all the Roman world. Restored today, the temple of Bacchus, with its towering Roman columns derived from Greek orders, is providing a dramatic setting for performances such as neither Roman nor Greek nor antique Syrian ever dreamed of. Opposite, the British prima ballerina Beryl Gray and her partner Bryan Ashbridge are seen opening a Baalbek Festival with a performance that includes dances from *Les Sylphides* and *Swan Lake*. This summer the Baalbek Festival, an extraordinary meeting of East and West, will open in July with an Old Vic production of *Macbeth* followed by a roster that will include Jean-Pierre Rampal's woodwind quartet and the Paris Opéra in a presentation of Gluck's neoclassic opera *Orfeo ed Euridice*.

ISRAEL OFFICE OF INFORMATION

Lunch at the Algonquin as drawn for HORIZON *by Al Hirschfeld: clockwise, foreground, Sherwood, Parker, Benchley, Woollcott; in rear, the Lunts, Crowninshield.*

High Spirits in the Twenties

A circle of young, exuberant wits (Robert Sherwood among them) regaled Dry-Era America from around a hotel table. Nothing quite like them has been seen since

By JOHN MASON BROWN

When Harding entered the postwar White House and Prohibition dried up the land, boatloads of disaffected intellectuals began taking off to ride out abroad what they regarded as an American cultural dark age. Yet enough of the youngest stayed at home to enliven it and each other. In the May, 1962, HORIZON *John Mason Brown ranged over the life of one of the most winning of these rising spirits in his "The Worlds of Robert Sherwood"; here, in pursuing his biography of the noted playwright, he follows young Sherwood as he enters New York fresh from battle in Canadian uniform to seek a fledgling editorial post and to find himself amid an array of talents as original as his own.*

On May 21, 1919, Robert Benchley, two days after he had taken over as managing editor of *Vanity Fair,* was writing in his diary about "meeting Bob Sherwood who presented his six feet five or ten in candidacy for a job he may get, as Miss Bristed is leaving." The postscript, as expected, is that Sherwood got the job and a week later was working at the office on a three-month trial basis at twenty-five dollars a week.

The pay was bread but not butter, the doors thrown open were large and wide, and the fun (for the eight months that it lasted) was larger still. "No young writer ever had such luck in starting his professional career in such fast company," Sherwood wrote years later to the author and actress Ilka Chase. *Vanity Fair* was the Gideon of the sophisticated. Frank Crowninshield was its boutonniere of an editor; Condé Nast, owner of the far more profitable but equally glossy *Vogue,* was its ducal and frugal publisher; and Sherwood's two associates, in whose office he was given a desk, were Robert Benchley and Dorothy Parker, with whom he at once formed an inseparable trio. The year was at the spring for Sherwood, and the lark on the wing, even if morning was seldom at seven. He was walking into the twenties under the most smiling and knowing of auspices.

Sherwood had impressed Crowninshield, and the office of *Vanity Fair* before Benchley was working there, by turning up as a job seeker resplendently attired in his kilted Black Watch uniform. Some may have thought that his doing this was poor taste; Sherwood thought it was good sense. Today's heroes become tomorrow's bores all too quickly. But when a war is just over, uniforms can open doors—and hearts. Crown-inshield was predictably responsive. His heart and Toscanini-bright eyes yielded to Sherwood. He knew the Sherwoods and knew of Robert from his work on the Harvard *Lampoon*, particularly the successful burlesque issue of *Vanity Fair*, which had appeared under Sherwood's editorship on April 6, 1917, of all days.

Crowninshield might with accuracy have borne the name of Fastidious Brisk, Ben Jonson's character. Few of his contemporaries had such charm, and none such a flair for the modish. When he walked down a side street, it turned into a boulevard. War, labor troubles, and scowling issues were not what he might have referred to as his métier. He was shallow of mind and deep of heart, constant in his enthusiasms, and better at private pleasantries than at public crises. He was not a hard-boiled egg, but a *soufflé* that could rise graciously to any and every occasion.

He wanted life to be charming, bubbly, and gay, and his magazine to be a cheerful and urbane month-by-month "record of current achievements in all the arts and a mirror of the progress and promise of American life." He liked dinner-table talk in print. As Benchley observed, he would allow any entertaining writer to say practically anything in *Vanity Fair* so long as he said it in evening clothes.

"Crownie" belonged to the old school and yet anticipated the new. A traditionalist, he was also an innovator. He bootlegged artistic Europe with success into an aesthetically dry United States. He was one of those who helped open America's at first somewhat baffled eyes to the beauties of modern art. He had a hazel-wand genius for discovering new, young talents. Warmhearted and politely impish, he liked the young because of his own lasting youth and welcomed their restrained impieties. He admired their freshness and did not object, any more than Nast did, to their being inexpensive.

He compared himself to a literary lion tamer, a Clyde Beatty of the ink-stained, confessing that in *Vanity Fair* he had found it always the safest plan "to deal with such felines when they are still cubs; to snare them, in traps, before their teeth have sharpened and their claws grown long." High on the lengthy list of *Vanity Fair* lions that he could, and did, point to with pride at a safe later distance were "those amazing whelps"—Dorothy Parker and Benchley and Sherwood.

Sherwood had first seen and heard Benchley at Harvard in the fall of 1914. He had gone to a freshman smoker, "a sort of get-together, good-will, beer-and-tobacco pep rally," designed to create college spirit in those who might otherwise have been devoting their energies to developing "Harvard indifference." The platform sagged under the weight of such football "greats" as Charlie Brickley and Eddie Mahan and Lev Saltonstall (later Governor and Senator). Yet there—and this gave Sherwood "a particular thrill"—costarred with them as if he were their equal, was Robert C. Benchley, of the class of 1912, a mere writer, cartoonist, actor, and merry-andrew, already so formidable by reputation that the freshmen "started laughing at the very mention of his name."

Robert Benchley laughed as he mimicked; Dorothy Parker used a stiletto

Since 1914 Benchley had been contributing to *Vanity Fair* under his own name and later also as "Brighton Perry." His pieces were "lampoonish" trifles, matured in expertness and successfully topsy-turvy. Indicative of what was to come was Benchley's first article, for which he was paid a lordly forty dollars. It was a moon-struck disquisition on the difficulties of writing a novel, the abrupt title of which was *No Matter From What Angle You Looked At It, Alice Brookhausen Was A Girl Whom You Would Hesitate To Invite Into Your Own Home.*

Benchley was to become stout as his fame, and as the decades accumulated, the writer in him seemed to be swallowed up in the actor celebrated for his humorous movie shorts. When he came to *Vanity Fair*, he was, as Crowninshield remembered, a pale young man who never had had a drink, was careful to wear long underwear, and was given to biting his nails. To Sherwood in those years Benchley seemed "a methodical, teetotaling, non-smoking, galosh-wearing, penurious, home-bound commuter, who didn't appear to have a worry or concern in the world beyond the precarious state of his bank account and the effect thereof on his family in Crestwood."

Sherwood soon came to know that this was only one character in the richly contrasted dramatis personae of Robert Benchley. The Benchley that Sherwood loved at once and found "forever wonderful to be with, to read about, and to remember," even in the later years when they did not see each other often, was subject to some of the strangest reversals of mood and habits that Sherwood had ever encountered in one human being. This was another bond between the two men, because the antitheses in Sherwood's nature were also abundant.

A dark room seemed to brighten when Benchley came into it. No one was readier to laugh than he, and few have ever been blessed with such a laugh. His laughter was an explosion of good humor. It was that rare thing—total laughter, ungrudging and with no joy withheld. It wrinkled his face into a contour map of pleasure, caused him to squint his twinkling blue eyes, thrust his head back, and shook his shoulders. It was from the belly and the heart as well as the head, and hope was always in it—the hope for a good joke—and the grace to pretend that a bad one had been good. He was a wit who had no malice in him. His gift for gaiety came to distress him as much as it always delighted others, for at heart he was a Stephen Leacock who was also a Baden-Powell, a moralist who wore the motley, and a do-gooder who could not persuade himself that creating such laughter as he did was a form of doing more good than it is given most to do.

He was a humorous writer and wanted to be a serious one. He liked to accuse himself of knowing little when, as a matter of fact, his knowledge was prodigious. He read as seriously as he wrote uproariously, dashing off such pieces as "The Social Life of the Newt" by day while reading Nietzsche or Henry

Adams by night—at least late at night. He devoured newspapers and magazines with a wolfing appetite and was uncommonly informed on the issues of the day—any day—and also on the trivia. He was a crusader for human rights, an earnest volunteer for the Urban League, a Puck who was to march in the picket lines for Sacco and Vanzetti, a dedicated pacifist, and, much to Sherwood's horror when he first knew him, an ardent prohibitionist—tone-deaf to the music of a cocktail shaker, though in time he became amply responsive to its rhythms.

Dorothy Parker had come to *Vanity Fair* in 1915 following a brief and uncomfortable sojourn on *Vogue* as Dorothy Rothschild, an elfin young woman, slim, sleek, and tiny, with masses of dark hair which, if not battened down by a large mushroom of a hat, seemed quite appropriately to be tornado-tossed. To Crowninshield she appeared reticent, self-effacing, and preternaturally shy.

Her smile was radiator warm; her manners perfect enough to have been suburban. But her tongue, which dripped honey, could also suddenly be asplike in its sting. Her eyes, laughing, thoughtful, and exceptionally luminous, were a curious mixture of hazel and green, and encircled by horn-rimmed spectacles that she removed abruptly if anyone spoke to her without warning. Her walk, in flat-heeled shoes or pumps with black bows, was short-stepped and quick. Her mind was quicker still.

To those she did not like or who bored her, she was a stiletto made of sugar. Her malice came from the disappointment of a romantic rather than the cynicism of the disillusioned. Delightful as it was to be in her presence, it was dangerous to leave it. Her epitaphs for the dear departed were widely repeated. She was to become not only a legend, treasured and feared, but a dictionary of quotations, many of which, with her annihilating wit, she had said or written herself but all of which, if they were witty or annihilating, were automatically attributed to her. In spite of her japeries, she, like Benchley and Sherwood, had a conscience ready to erupt and the courage to back up what she fiercely felt.

The year before Sherwood turned up at *Vanity Fair*, Miss Rothschild had become Mrs. Parker when she married Edwin Parker, a lifelong friend from Connecticut. If her apprenticeship of writing captions for *Vogue* had been brief, it was because she chose to dash off for a page display of undergarments such a caption as "Brevity is the Soul of Lingerie, as the Petticoat said to the Chemise." Thereby she made it clear to those in authority that "fashion would never become a religion with her," and Crowninshield claimed her at a small salary for *Vanity Fair*. After the Armistice, as a bride waiting for her husband's return from France, she had become the magazine's drama editor, having already won a name for herself by baring her claws in "A Hate Song" she had addressed to Men. Of herself she said:

> *But I, despite expert advice,*
> *Keep doing things I think are nice,*
> *And though to good I never come—*
> *Inseparable my nose and thumb.*

Her nose and thumb were already in position when Sherwood became a triple pillar of that small unconventional office at *Vanity Fair*. At first Benchley and Mrs. Parker may have thought, as Crowninshield believed, that Sherwood was "pretty fast." He wore his straw hat at a roguish angle. He made dates with the beautiful receptionist. He had lived a soldier's life in Canada, France, and England, and "had once, perhaps inadvertently, referred to a personal hangover."

In no time their acquaintanceship became a friendship, their friendship a federation. They were young. They wrote with youth's plunging facility. A conquerable thing called "life" lay not only ahead of them but all around them. They loved to laugh, and in one another's company found plenty to laugh about. Although serious too, they doted on pranks and planned them as solemnly as if they had been drafting State of the Union messages. Crowninshield's conviction was that at no period of their lives did they find "more enjoyment, make more friends, or work as hard or as easily."

When Nast was away, there were beginnings of high play

In a moment of rashness Crowninshield and Nast had sailed for Europe, leaving the publication of two issues of *Vanity Fair* to "Mr. Benchley" and his assistants, "Mrs. Parker" and "Mr. Sherwood." Not only was the High Command in Europe but the conductor of the magazine's "For the Well-Dressed Man" department went on vacation, leaving behind a column only half-written, which Sherwood was asked to complete. He set about the job gleefully, filling the page (which he was confident no one ever read) with such bizarre predictions for male fashions as, "*On dit* that peg-topped pants and cloth-top shoes are coming back; also that the best-dressed man's next year's waistcoats will glitter darkly with cut jade." At least one person did read the column—its regular editor, and he was not amused. He came back raging.

When Crowninshield and Nast returned from Europe at the end of August, the "cat's away" trio were sorry to have their holiday of work over but glad to see "Crownie." They spent some time scurrying around town to get the most garish decorations they could find, including banners and crepe paper, to welcome him home to his office. But little by little, it was becoming clear that they were misfits in the hothouse atmosphere of the organization. Although they were zealous workers when they got to work, they did not believe in their having to be at their desks at 9. Nast did, as firmly as he believed in salaries constant in their smallness. He was a routineer; they were last-minute inspirationists. As an executive, he had ideas about efficiency that were baffling to them. The frequent ukases issued by his office manager, Francis L. Wurzburg, were not for them edicts but invitations to revolt.

There was, for instance, the "Policy Memorandum" requiring tardy employees to explain their lateness on cards. It delighted Sherwood to recall the conscientiousness with which Benchley one morning complied with this regulation. His explanation, which covered the card, its margins, and its back with the most minute writing, had to do with his having been detained by rounding up a herd of elephants that had escaped from the Hippodrome, with the result that he was eleven minutes late getting to the office. This was his last tardy slip.

There was that other "Policy Memorandum" forbidding "discussion among employees of salary received." This was answered by Sherwood, Benchley, and Mrs. Parker with prompt and deserved contempt. Not limiting themselves to a hotly worded written protest, they made placards, on which their salaries were printed large, and paraded through the office wearing them. This put an abrupt end to another commandment.

Where there had been happiness, there came friction, apprehension, and anger. The sound of a snickersnee being sharpened was in the air. By early January in 1920, the light-hearted threesome was, according to Benchley's diary, "waxing very low." They suspected that Sherwood was "on the verge of being canned" and knew that Mrs. Parker's pittance had not been upped at the first of the year. The spirits of the three inseparables so drooped that before Sherwood and Mrs. Parker learned their fates, they had at a little tea at Henri's "all but decided to tell the Nast Co. to do what it could with itself." Even the ebullient Benchley was in a "to-hell-with-everything" mood. The ax fell on Sherwood the next day.

The Algonquin Table-Round is formed; the chiefs take places

In May, 1920, "Mrs. Parker," "Mr. Benchley," and "Mr. Sherwood" again found themselves together in New York, only this time they were without *Vanity Fair*. In their months on the magazine they had grown accustomed to lunching and dining together so as not to interrupt the serial that was their conversation. Naturally, they had sought some welcoming and agreeable place nearby. *Vanity Fair* was at 19 West Forty-fourth Street. Had men's clubs in those days augmented their income by admitting women, the three might have gone to the Harvard Club a few doors away, as Benchley and Sherwood did when Mrs. Parker was not with them. Since she generally was, they got in the habit of going a little farther down the block to the Algonquin.

The trio were not alone in finding the Algonquin a beckoning place, nor did they by any means discover it. Since its opening in 1902, it had had a magnet's tug for writers, theatre people, and the stage-struck. Though a hotel, the Algonquin had come to have all the endearing attributes of an inn. Always too small, with its one elevator for passengers rising and descending as sleepily as if awakened from a nap, it was an Edwardian reminder that certain fundamentals of comfort are beyond the whims of decorators. When Sherwood, Benchley, and Mrs. Parker found themselves among its new habitués, the Algonquin was not so much an old-fashioned place as a place settled, long lived in, and loved. Some likened it to Brown's Hotel in London, Louis Bromfield to old Frau Sacher's, about which Sherwood was to write in *Reunion in Vienna*. It did not need a welcome mat. "Welcome" was in the air.

There were plenty of other hotels and restaurants in the Broadway neighborhood that might have won the theatre's trade and the legendary name that came to the Algonquin in the twenties. But none of these had Frank Case as master of the inn. He was the one who persuaded his boss, its builder and first proprietor, not to call the hotel the Puritan but the Algonquin, because a visit to the Public Library had revealed to him that the Algonquins were the first and strongest people in the neighborhood. Some argued that the new tribe, which moved in with the establishment of the Round Table, used tomahawks with inherited skill and were also master scalpers.

Case was the ideal Boniface for a hotel that catered to actors and writers. A lean, spruce man, pale of face but warm of heart, he had a somewhat beakish nose, a thin mustache over thin, smiling lips, and twinkling eyes that radar-swept a room, spotting at once the important persons who were present. His social register was *Who's Who in the Theatre*. Big-business men, social leaders, and politicians did not impress him. Writers, musicians, painters, and particularly people of the theatre did. They were different, set apart, special. From the outset he was determined to attract them. What is more, he did. His firm belief was that gifted people, more than being tolerated, should be encouraged "in their strange and temperamental antics." This belief was his policy at the Algonquin. He had the listener's gift and, as a measure of his patience, tact, and absorption, was as truly interested in hearing a performer talk about his performance as the actor was. He coddled egos with the skill of his chef coddling eggs. He welcomed individuality, an invitation his patrons accepted, and none more willingly than those men and women who in 1919 began to assemble at what came to be known as the Round Table.

The Round Table was an improvisation that turned into a habit and in the process became a force and then a myth. Always blessedly free of officers, bylaws, attendance requirements, dues, and a gavel, it stumbled into being when a number of individuals, many of whom were accustomed to eating frequently at the Algonquin, started lunching there more or less as a group day after day, and continued to do so for about a decade.

The initial impromptu gatherings were in the long, side room, now called the Oak Room but then known as the Pergola. Case, a shrewd publican, was quick to realize the value of having so many publicists at his inn, mentioning it in their columns while mentioning each other. He moved them into the Rose Room, his main dining room at the back of the lobby, placing them at a table near the entrance. As the attendance increased, he moved them again in the same room, this time to a large circular table upstage center. At it, and at neighboring tables if there was an overflow, these "celebrities"—real, small, large, or self-imagined—were on exhibition, and as they grew in fame, more and more people came daily to stare at them at their round table.

At first the group was as nameless as a foundling. Then some of its members began to refer to it jokingly as "The Board." When a waiter named Luigi was assigned to them, this became inescapably "The Luigi Board." From that they proceeded with delight to "The Vicious Circle." In *Black Oxen* Gertrude Atherton within a few years referred to them as "The Sophisticates." Their enemies, in whom they were rich, were from the beginning less kind. They called them, among other things, "The Log Rollers." To many they were, and remained, "The Algonquin Group." To more they were known as "The Round Table," because of the cartoon Edmund Duffy of the Brooklyn *Eagle* drew of them as knights in armor sitting at their round table. They would have been the first to admit that there was nothing Arthurian about them except the shape of the table Case reserved for them.

They were a glittering lot, these men and women with whom Sherwood began to lunch almost daily. All of them were young in spirit, and most of them in fact. Sherwood, twenty-four, was within months of being the youngest, and the next to oldest by a year was Franklin Pierce Adams, thirty-eight, better known because of his *Tribune* column, "The Conning Tower," as F.P.A. Those who already had reputations were on the verge of adding to them. The majority of those who did not were about to make them. In or out of print, in the theatre or in the glare of columns, they were to move increasingly into the spotlight as the twenties progressed. The journalists among them, by quoting their cronies or mentioning them in print, saw to it that they were not dogged by obscurity. To the delight not of all but of many, including themselves, they became the town's ruling wits, and theirs was a lively rule.

Among the faithful or fitful in their Round Table attendance were, in addition to Sherwood and F.P.A., Woollcott, Heywood Broun, Benchley, Marc Connelly, George S. Kaufman, Frank Sullivan, Donald Ogden Stewart, Deems Taylor, Howard Dietz, Harold Ross, Laurence Stallings, John V. A. Weaver, Russel Crouse, John T. Winterich, John Peter Toohey, David Wallace, Hawley Truax, and the two Pembertons, Brock and Murdock. The women included Edna Ferber (when she was willing to take time off from her writing), Margaret Leech (a regular because she had an office next door), Alice Duer Miller (an intermittent visitor), Ruth Hale, Beatrice Kaufman, Jane Grant, Neysa McMein (very rarely present), Alison Smith, Mary Brandon (who was to figure in Sherwood's life), Ruth Gordon, Peggy Wood, Margalo Gillmore, and, of course, Mrs. Parker. Actually about ten people were apt to lunch each day at the Round Table. Guests who accepted an invitation to join them ran a risk not covered by insurance. To survive in this company, outsiders had to be armed and armored.

To say what a thing is not is an approach to saying what it is. Among those who were not members of the Round Table were Ernest Hemingway, Stephen Vincent Benet, Willa Cather, Eugene O'Neill, Edna St. Vincent Millay, Sinclair Lewis, Elinor Wylie, Theodore Dreiser, Sherwood Anderson, F. Scott Fitzgerald, Thornton Wilder, John P. Marquand, Thomas Wolfe, Don Marquis, Christopher Morley, Walter Lippmann, Mencken and Nathan, Lewis Mumford, Stark Young, Joseph Wood Krutch, Edmund Wilson, Malcolm Cowley, Carl and Mark Van Doren, Gilbert Seldes, Percy Hammond, Norman Bel Geddes, and Robert Edmond Jones. These, by their absence, help to define the nature and concerns of those present. Some of the unincluded were occasional visitors; others were greatly admired by the group; still others, by temperament and cast of mind, were utterly alien to it.

The Tablers did not meet as candidates for the Poets' Corner, political pundits, members of a Faculty Club, or as lily-claspers made grave by beauty. Among them Benchley no more discussed the notes he was making for a serious study of the humorists of Queen Anne's day than F.P.A. recited Horace in Latin, or than Sherwood thought of mentioning his reading of Livy, Juvenal, and Mommsen in preparation for his *The Road to Rome*. They did not meet in public to be solemn.

When pundits unite, someone is likely to get hurt—or left out

To their delight and the delight of those who could hear them only when their sallies were reported in print, theirs was frequently the comedy of bad manners. They were wisecrackers, more apt to use the bludgeon than the rapier, who often spoke not to encourage further talk but to silence what had gone before. Their malice could be greater than their mercy. What they were able to give, they expected others to be prepared to take. They knew a good line when they heard—or said—one and were as warm in their respect for the mots of others as for their own. Conversationally they stalked each other, waiting for the chance to fire the topping gag. This required, as Case's daughter, Margaret Case Harriman, noted in her charmingly evocative *The Vicious Circle*, "a miraculous sense of timing" because "with them, a joke had one chance, and one only." "A Round Tabler," she pointed out, "might treasure for a half an hour a remark he had thought up, chatting amiably meanwhile, and then, in the space of an indrawn breath, expel it into precisely the right moment of silence." Although, according to her, "they were all born hams, in the most lovable sense of the word," the writers oddly enough were more expert at this split-timing than the actors.

If insults were their favorite weapons for demolishing adversaries, or even those guilty only of inanity, nonsense was one of the ways in which they made sense. To the charge sometimes brought against them that they worked too hard at being wits, they could have answered, as Charles Lamb did, that trying to be witty is at least as good as aiming at dullness.

With that ginny, smoky, delectable little man, they had another thing in common. They loved puns. They loved them as much as all people dislike them who cannot make them. They were not among the witless who dismiss them as the lowest form of wit. They knew that there is no such thing as stooping to a pun. There is the challenge of rising to a good one or appreciating a bad one, if only it is bad enough and meant to be so. Their puns, such as Kaufman's "One man's Mede is another man's Persian," Peggy Wood's "Well, back to the mimes" when returning to a rehearsal, Woollcott's saying at cards "I'll fold up my tens and silently steal away," Sherwood's "Only the brave *chemin de fer,*" Frank Adams's solving the problem of building a sentence around "meretricious" with "Meretricious 'n' a Happy New Year," and Mrs. Parker's solving the same problem with "horticulture" by coming up with "You may lead a whore to culture but you can't make her think"—these and a hundred others of their kind may by now have become enfeebled by familiarity. But they were born of a moment, and meant for that moment, and at that moment they were triumphant. Rob a pun of the moment of its first being made, and no matter how good it may remain, it has already lost something. As Lamb knew, "a pun has a hearty kind of ear-kissing smack in it; you can no more transmit it than you can send a kiss."

The Round Tablers' brightness was of a kind that caused many to squint, some to view them through the darkest of dark glasses, and others to turn away entirely. Being gay, they seemed frivolous to the serious, and having the power that came from print and success, they irritated those who resented their influence.

George M. Cohan, upon whose Broadway they poached, described them as "A Round Table without a square man at it." Then there were those who dismissed them, or tried to do so, as a coterie of exhibitionists and back-scratchers and deplored their manners (as if they all shared Woollcott's) and ridiculed their tastes. Decades later the very memory of them in their heyday stuck in the craw of Marquand. With a fine mustering of spleen, some of it unfeigned, he recalled them as "a lot of conceited second-raters" whose pranks were as intolerable as their assumptions of intellectual superiority. As late as January, 1959, Ben Hecht and, of all people, Mrs. Parker were attacking them on a television show. Hecht damned them as "a remarkable unit of illiteracy"; Mrs. Parker, the most quoted of their jesters, complained of "their little jokes all about themselves," and contended, her memory playing odd tricks upon her, that "none of them had read anything written before 1920. Most of them," she said, "are dead now, but they weren't too alive then." They were, however, alive enough to make New York for a decade a far livelier place than it was before, or has been since, by what they wrote and did and because of what they were.

On those occasions, and for us they *were* occasions, when we who were still younger went to the Rose Room, we could not at our side tables hear what was being said by those men and women whose plays and performances we were seeing; whose books, columns, and reviews we devoured; and who seemed to us the embodiment of Times Square sophistication, gaiety, and success. We could only gape at them and hear their distant laughter and be hopefully certain that what they laughed at was the ultimate in wit and drollery. We were not

alone in feeling this. Countless older New Yorkers, also avid readers of "the page opposite" in the *World*, felt as we did, and so did out-of-towners beyond numbering who flocked to the Algonquin as part of their Broadway pilgrimage.

The Algonquin galaxy grows, and some of its stars are variables

Sherwood took to these men and women, and they to him, just as he took to the world to which they introduced him. They were molding influences and examples. In them he found the echoes of his hopes and needs, and reflections of himself, or diversion and companionship. They were not like him, but like enough to be near to him, or sufficiently different to amuse him. In their dissimilar ways they fitted into the intricate cloisonné of his character, and most of them were to remain his friends even when he and they, in Alice's fashion, had moved on to different squares.

Woollcott, for example, of whom Sherwood was fond and who was fond of Sherwood, was, to the relief of some, like no one else. He sported his personality like a blazer and rejoiced in being unmuffled by those restraints to which most submit. The man who came to lunch was in many respects already the man who was to come to dinner. Even then he was sitting for a preliminary sketch of Sheridan Whiteside, the character who was to dominate George S. Kaufman's hilarious comedy. Portly as a matron, he was inevitably caricatured as an owl because of the roundness of his face, the swoop of his small nose, and the thick, large glasses through which he stared.

Kaufman, once asked to summarize him in a word, thought hard and said, "Improbable." That was what Woollcott was in his appearance, gifts, and contradictions. A sizzling mixture of arsenic and treacle, he was as warm in his resentments as in his enthusiasms. He was an actor who was forever playing one or the other of his two favorite parts: "a much uplifted onlooker" or "an old meanie." When Sherwood first knew him, his daily reviews for the New York *Times*, next the *Herald*, then the *World*, may not have been criticism, but they were performances, Woollcott performing so that the emotions of a first night were captured in print with an immediacy unmatched in our times.

Phalanx, New Jersey, where he was born; Hamilton College, to which he went; the mumps, which came to him when he was a young man; and the First World War, during which he served overseas on *Stars and Stripes* with Adams and Ross, were among the abiding influences on Woolcott—these and the theatre in terms of which he was always to see life. A "perhapsless" man, he could be the equal in sentimentality of James Barrie's McConnachie or downright feline in the swiftness of his scratch. He loved wonder, coincidence, murders, anecdotes, rags-to-riches yarns, trivia, and suspense, and was able in his talk and writing to convey his infatuation with them.

Naturally he had his enemies, but he rejoiced in them, even as he did in his no less numerous friends, whom as the years progressed and he became a part of the public domain, he sometimes seemed to choose as much for his reader's enjoyment as his own. He was a "curmudgeon," though not the "bogus" one he liked to describe himself as being. He had the courage of his eccentricities, his whims, his indifferent taste, and his misbehavior. Though he gave pain, he gave pleasure, and much of it to Sherwood. The two of them were to watch one another's changing careers with interest and admiration.

Franklin Pierce Adams, with whom Sherwood also enjoyed talk and cards and companionship, was not so noisy a bully as Woollcott, but he too was intimidating, and even Woollcott deferred to him. His was a scowling, prowling, dusklike Armenian face that suddenly became noontime in the brightness of its smiles. A dead pan at one moment, it radiated life at the next and was made winning by the fullness of its participation. F.P.A.'s cone-shaped head was topped by black hair that had the look of steel wool—used, scratchy, and rusty. His nose was a promontory, his mustache a shaded cove, and his chin somewhat in retreat from his lower lip, which had a gargoyle's outward thrust. His ugliness was readily forgotten, however, because of the wrinkles of recognition that without warning would animate his features and the unpredictable blaze of his small, dark, closely spaced eyes as they lit his witticisms on their way. He was a curator of taste, passionate in his concern for the purities of the language and blessed (or cursed) with a proofreader's eye for correction. Though he delighted in seeming grumpy or gruff, he was essentially kind and could be beguiling.

Heywood Broun, more than seven years older than Sherwood, came to be involved sooner than the latter in serious causes but, in what was to be Sherwood's fashion, combined ardent commitment with the gift for gaiety. Widely loved and widely loving, Broun was feared for his indignation and treasured for his humor. On the undulant acreage that was his face, his precise, pointed nose struggled to be recognized. His hands were balloon-large, and among his ample curves were his thumbs, which bent wristward as if weighted down by prodigality. His small dark eyes fought against the flesh that encircled them but never against the laughter within them or the kindness. His body was mountainous like his inner abundance, his clothes always a range of wrinkles. Finding images for his sloppiness was easy sport. Someone likened him to "an unmade bed," another to "a one-man slum," and Peggy Bacon to "a stage elephant made of two men."

A sentimentalist (in his phrase "an easy weeper") and a wit, Broun was also an extravagant champion, a formidable foe, and a crusader whose indignation, when aroused as in his defense of Sacco and Vanzetti, blazed forth with passion and without restraint. He had the facility of the naturally humorous and the eloquence of strong feelings. An able sports writer when Sherwood first knew him, Broun soon became a diverting theatrical reviewer and then a powerful, freewheeling columnist. Untidy in his turbulence, he tried painting, novel writing, and biography, too, and in time helped organize the Newspaper Guild. Although he hated to approach a typewriter, he was miraculously swift when at the last moment he sat down before one. He had only contempt for commentators whose search was for the right word rather than the just cause. He never had to search for either.

The theatre, a fever in the bloodstream of the twenties, was an epidemic among the Round Tablers. Most of them were seized with the desire to write plays, and sooner or later, in Sherwood's fashion, most of them did, with sweet-moneyed and garlanded success. Chief among the carriers were two of their own number, Kaufman and Marc Connelly, who spread the contagion by turning to playwrighting early and making it seem easy by the series of hits they produced. From 1921 to 1924, from *Dulcy* and *To the Ladies* to *Merton of the Movies* and *The Beggar on Horseback*, Kaufman and Connelly were Broadway's favored Siamese twins, collaborators as linked in the public mind as Gilbert and Sullivan or, for that matter, as Kaufman and Moss Hart were to be in the thirties. Although thought of during these budding years as if they were one person because of the deceptive blend their comedies seemed to be, they were glaringly dissimilar.

"Marcus," or even "Marcus Parcus," as Connelly was sometimes called affectionately by those whose lives and living rooms he brightened, was a plump, Pickwickian man, already bald, whose nose rose from his face like the pointer on a sundial. He was a Winnie-the-Pooh grown up, protean within himself and protean in what he could become. Inhibitions did not shackle him nor audiences large or small dismay him. An author who contained an actor, he was an actor who enclosed a professor.

Radiantly gifted as a mimic, as good at improvising as at remembering, he could, without bothering about props or costumes, be Spartacus at one moment and at the next either Barbara Frietchie waving her rebel flag or Ruth Draper serving coffee at a railway lunch counter on the Western plains. He could lift a party as few could and drop it only when the "Herr Doktor" in him took over or he arrived too fresh from a reading of the encyclopedia. He worked rapidly and well, once he got started, but his imagination was such that he could mistake the intention to work for work already done. Woollcott, who came to respect him hugely, called him an "infuriating blend of poet, peacock, and procrastinator." Connelly was more than that, far more, as Sherwood realized when once he defended him against Woollcott's charge that he would never get anything done after the Kaufman-Connelly partnership dissolved. His *Green Pastures* lay ahead.

Kaufman was in many respects Connelly's antonym. All nerves and concentration, he was as lean and tense as an exclamation point. His face was long, his patience short. His black hair rose like a cliff from his expansive forehead, his chin had cement in it, his nose was large and imperious, his cheekbones were as high as an Indian chief's, and his dark eyes burned behind his tortoise-shell glasses like coals banked deeply in a grate. A tireless worker, he was a craftsman who labored over the fashioning of a line or scene until both functioned with the accuracy of precision instruments.

Shyness was at the core of Kaufman's being. Friendship with him was not easy, though many, in Sherwood's fashion, found it well worth the difficulties. He could—and did—write letters in which he expressed the kind of warm appreciation of people that he was incapable of stating face to face. He writhed when complimented and cringed at betrayals of emotion. He himself was often seized and touched emotionally—as Moss Hart came to know and said in *Act One,* that most successful of theatrical success stories—and was as susceptible as the next fellow "to the dark doubts which licked other men's souls." But he fought a winning battle to keep his stronger feelings hidden. As Hart observed, "He was not driven by a savage necessity to be liked." He had his own standards, was indifferent to the good opinions of others, kowtowed to no one, and could be dispatchingly abrupt. His wit, which won him wide respect, also caused him to be widely feared, and made even Woollcott uneasy in his presence.

Out of the Round Table endlessly rocking, a major playwright

Among these Round Tablers, Sherwood stood out like a grandfather's clock. The tick of his talk was measured, his words seeming to be spaced by minutes, but when he chimed he struck gaily. What was deepest in him had, except when he wrote, a hard time getting out. Although his likes and dislikes were strong and he could say sharp things, he took no pleasure in wounding and was not among the scrappers. The slowness of his speech was his tongue's guardian in such fast-talking company. His silences were often his retorts, his somewhat tortured smiles his signals of enjoyment, and his looks of incredulity the register of his mustering disapproval.

He had much of Benchley's gentleness and not a little of Kaufman's shyness. At times he had a disquieting way of being absent, though present, and at other times of suddenly joining in as a jubilant participant. He was not at all shy when it came to the parlor games at which the group excelled, nor to public speaking, radio appearances, acting, singing, or dancing. In spite of the misery on his face while performing, he reveled in all these displays, being, as he confessed, "just a frustrated actor, exercising vicariously an exhibition complex."

Sherwood, who seldom forgot anything, whether it was history, a book, a newspaper story, a place, a play, a performance, or a chance remark made during dinner, had a memory of old songs and the lyrics of mildewed musicals that was staggering. Nor did he mind sharing this knowledge. He sang and danced these numbers as if he were composing the Gettysburg Address, but he loved doing them. From the mid-twenties on—when first, at a family party with his young nephew James Townsend, he strutted and sang his way in blackface through "When the Red, Red Robin Comes Bob, Bob, Bobbin' Along"—he took over this Jolson song until it became his signature. In his later and last years a party was not a party for him, and therefore for his friends, until he,

this brooding man, was happy enough (the blackface long since omitted) to reach for a hat and cane and plunge into his routine, his long arms and legs twirling like the sails of a windmill in a hurricane.

Due to his gravity, young Sherwood appeared to be older than he was. The pain he had known in the war was on his face, and so was the distress the peace had brought him. He approached the Round Table welcoming the armistice of laughter its members and their friends gave him but not forgetting the troubled world beyond this special one. There was something about this older-young man that even at twenty-four inspired confidence and confidences. Among the many who felt this, was a young Milwaukee-born actor named Alfred Lunt, who had just captured New York by his comic excellence in Booth Tarkington's *Clarence.* Lunt was convinced on meeting him that Sherwood was three years his senior when, as a matter of fact, he was three years Lunt's junior. At their first lunch together Lunt found himself telling Sherwood, as most decidedly he had not intended to, that he was very much in love with an English actress, Lynn Fontanne. She was then making her name in Laurette Taylor's company and would soon establish herself in *Dulcy,* the merry comedy which Kaufman and Connelly were to build around Dulcinea, that queen of bromides in F.P.A.'s column.

Naturally, in such a world Sherwood was bound to try his hand at writing a play. He had been writing plays since childhood and had come to the Round Table fresh from the deceptive amateur success of *Barnum Was Right* at Harvard's Hasty Pudding. What the others could do, and were doing, he would do. The doing was not to be as easy as he thought. By 1922 he had dashed off a happily forgotten script, *The Dawn Man,* "actually my first play," he was to say, meaning for professional production; but it was "so dreadful" that it caused him to abandon playwriting as a career.

Not for long, however. The Tablers continued to tempt him by example—in particular, Laurence Stallings, that exuberant ex-Marine captain who had lost a leg at Belleau Wood. Two years after Sherwood's abortive attempt, Stallings with Maxwell Anderson, an editorial writer for the *World,* had written *What Price Glory?* With rapture Sherwood listened to the applause and cheers, loud as a bombardment, that greeted this lusty play which, as Woollcott recognized, said more, without editorializing, about "the war, its immensity, and its crushing evidence of human failure" than all the editorials on the subject.

In 1936, when the clouds of a second war were lowering, Sherwood, with the long since married Alfred Lunt and Lynn Fontanne, stirred another first-night audience to comparable enthusiasm with another anti-war play. At the curtain's fall on *Idiot's Delight* he "rushed backstage and thrilled to the sounds of the greatest demonstration any play of mine has ever received. Nineteen curtain calls, vociferous cheers—what I have been hoping for ever since I saw *What Price Glory?* twelve years ago, and decided it would be wonderful to be a playwright."

Director Kurosawa at work on the set of **The Magnificent Seven**

Akira Kurosawa was once described as "the most complicated man in films: completely Japanese and, so far as the West is concerned, almost completely Western." Since his debut as a motion-picture director in 1943, he has been called an idealist and a realist, a typical Japanese intellectual and an American-type fact-finder. He has been defended as a humanist and attacked as a despot. In 1951, when a producer demanded that Kurosawa cut his three-hour-and-ten-minute film *The Idiot,* the director snapped back, "If you want to cut it in half, you had better cut it lengthwise." His penchant for making such retorts has earned him the derisive sobriquet of Kurosawa-*Tenno*, "The Emperor Kurosawa."

In spite of the difficulty critics have in placing Kurosawa in the East or the West (and perhaps partially because of that difficulty) his ferociously guarded independence, his spirited experimentation, and his vigorous break from traditional Japanese film standards have won him an esteem about which there is little argument: he is considered one of the best directors Japan has produced; indeed, in the opinion of many critics he is one of the world's foremost. Public recognition first came to him in 1948 with the appearance of *Drunken Angel,* and by 1951 his *Rashomon* won the Venice Film Festival Grand Prix, the Academy Award for Best Foreign Film, and prizes from the National Board of Review and the New York Film Critics Group.

Born in Tokyo in 1910, Kurosawa developed an early in-

DOSTOEVSKY WITH
A JAPANESE CAMERA

Akira Kurosawa applies Western philosophy to

Eastern themes in films that appeal—if not

always for the same reasons—to both worlds

By DONALD RICHIE

terest in painting—a taste that is reflected in the emphasis on pictorial beauty in his films—and while still in his teens he attended a private Western-style art school. However, when he found he could not make a living by painting, he began to look for a job. In 1936, with a minimum of enthusiasm, he responded to a newspaper advertisement for an assistant director at Photo-Chemical Laboratory, one of Japan's first movie-producing companies (now called Toho). He got the job, largely owing to an essay he was required to write. With characteristic rebelliousness he chose as his subject: "What Is Wrong with Japanese Movies."

For the next seven years Kurosawa worked as an assistant on several films and spent most of his spare time writing scenarios (none of which was then produced); finally, in 1943, he directed his first film, *Sanshiro Sugata*. It dealt with a young judo champion who pursues the Buddhist ideal, and strives for enlightenment—the perfection of his spirit—through a rigorous physical discipline. The most notable aspect of the film, however, was the early indication it gave of the style that characterizes much of Kurosawa's work: the scenes follow one another relentlessly, switching abruptly from "stillness" to action and back again.

This tightly-woven style, more fully developed, is used to good effect in *Rashomon*, Kurosawa's most widely known film. The plot of *Rashomon* is simple. A samurai and his bride meet a bandit in the woods. The samurai is murdered, the girl is raped, and the events are witnessed by a wood-cutter. The film consists of four separate versions of the story, each depending on the viewpoint of the person telling it. According to the girl, she was raped against her will; according to the bandit, he was lured by her and persuaded to kill her husband. As the personal motives are unmasked, it becomes apparent that there is no "true" version: truth, like beauty, lies in the eye of the beholder. Yet Kurosawa was not content to end with unresolved despair (he finds distasteful the ordinary Japanese film with its "almost obligatory unhappy ending")—and so he added an epilogue in which the woodcutter adopted an abandoned child.

In *Rashomon*, Kurosawa shows his characteristic interest in violence, action of the most heightened order, and the use of the camera itself to achieve dramatic effects. In the opening forest sequence the moving camera looks straight through leaves into the sun to make palpable the glare and shade on the samurai and his lady. Such effects are achieved by painstaking work and the director's absolute control over all phases of a production. Ten feet of film are shot for every one that finds its way onto the screen, and Kurosawa uses two or three cameras to photograph the same scene from different angles. He carefully plots each perspective, and he is one of the few directors who insists upon the right to "frame" his own scenes. Unlike many directors, he cuts and edits the footage himself.

To insure unity of mood in his adaptation of Gorky's *The Lower Depths* (*Donzoko*, 1957, released in America in Feb-

In making Rashomon, *Kurosawa broke with Japanese tradition and introduced a full-blooded story, bold pictorial imagery, and the savagely realistic acting of, for example, this duel between a samurai (left) and an outlaw for possession of the farmer's lady.*

RASHOMON (1950)

ruary of this year)—a difficult feat when transferring a play to a different country and a different era—Kurosawa ordered a forty-day rehearsal period with full costumes in use from the first day. It was an unusual demand from a film maker, but it produced an admirable, consistent, ensemble effect.

One of Kurosawa's most arresting displays of technical virtuosity was *Throne of Blood* (*Kumonosu-jo,* 1957, shown in America in 1961), in which he transplanted Shakespeare's *Macbeth* to medieval Japan. In Kurosawa's version of the story, Lady Macbeth's influence is only incidental: Macbeth is given full responsibility for his actions. In technique, too, there are numerous inventions, one of the most striking being the director's experiment with the sound track. Kurosawa turned off all the "highs" so that the voices would be masculine and gruff. Indeed, they often sound more animal than human. There is a stunning scene in which hundreds of birds, disturbed by the destruction of their forest, fly into the banquet hall, considerably unnerving the hero. Then, when the couple speaks of the murder and of sleeplessness, the sound of a horse in the courtyard, galloping endlessly round and round in a circle, heightens the dialogue. The march of the forest on the castle is photographed in slow motion, distorted by the use of a telescopic lens, with trees swaying like gigantic seaweed and descending wave after wave upon the castle. The conclusion is an almost ritualistic murder of Macbeth when, arrow by arrow (and there are hundreds of them), he is immolated.

The technical effects Kurosawa employed in *The Record of a Living Being* (*Ikimono-no Kiroku,* 1955) were also startlingly appropriate. In this film Kurosawa tells the story of a man obsessed with the fear of atomic extinction. The man attempts to move his family to Brazil, where he believes they will find safety, but the family, complacent and cynical, succeeds in having him judged insane. Eventually he does become insane, and we see him in the asylum, looking at the sun and believing the earth is finally on fire.

Set in the hottest days of August, the atmosphere of a brutal summer permeates *Record of a Living Being:* clothes stick to the flesh, characters fan themselves incessantly, and in the corner of most interior shots there is an electric fan stirring the heavy air, providing more noise and irritation than relief. A flickering, disquieting motion is present in every scene. During one of the climactic moments, Kurosawa places the camera so that the pages of a magazine, blown by an electric fan, confuse and fatigue the spectator with their incessant and meaningless motion. The camera, like the hero, peers myopically at objects like telephones and typewriters until they become huge and menacing.

In the final scene, in the asylum, the camera sets itself between floors, one flight of stairs leading up, the other down. The doctor, an old man who has been sympathetic toward the mad hero, goes down the stairs, passing but not recognizing the young man's mistress, who is carrying a baby upstairs—possibly the hero's child—for a visit. This conclud-

Kurosawa worked modern ideas and dialogue into the sixteenth-century setting of The Magnificent Seven, *a romantic tale of war and comradeship, in which seven samurai warriors defend a remote farming village against a troop of armed bandits.*

THE MAGNIFICENT SEVEN (1953–54)

ing comment of rebirth has been a persistent theme in Kurosawa's films; and it suggests, along with less tangible influences, the contribution of the director's early interest in Dostoevsky.

Kurosawa read *The Idiot* and *Crime and Punishment* over and over again as a youngster, and Dostoevsky's imprint was unmistakable in even the first of his major films, *Drunken Angel* (*Yoidore Tenshi,* 1948, shown in America in 1959). The film tells the story of an alcoholic doctor who finds a tubercular young hoodlum and attempts to nurse him back to health. The gangster is almost as afraid of the doctor as he is of the disease. The doctor, already a failure, insists on saving this apparently worthless young man; the young man, also a failure in his own world, feels that salvation at the hands of someone who so attracts and repels him would represent defeat. Their mutual antagonism, a parable on the responsibilities of compassion, is set in the ruins of postwar Japan, where social and ethical norms have been completely destroyed, and where an entire society lies helpless and festering. Kurosawa once said of Dostoevsky, "I know of no one so compassionate . . . ordinary people turn their eyes away from tragedy; he looks straight into it."

Intended as a comment on postwar Japan, an effort to revive the spirit of that decimated country, *Drunken Angel* received the "Best One" award from the Japanese film magazine *Kinema Jumpo,* and Kurosawa followed it with a similar comment in *Stray Dog* (*Nora Inu,* 1949, not commercially shown in America). In this film a detective pursues a seasoned criminal who has stolen a pistol and committed a number of murders. When the cop finally catches the robber (and there is a "cops and robbers" feeling about this film, a detective story of the classic genre), they fight among the flowering weeds of early spring. Completely covered with mud, finally exhausted by their fight, the two lie side by side. Then the camera, for the first time dropping its aloof and dispassionate documentary attitude, peers curiously at them through the blossoms and finds them identical. Muddy and unrecognizable, lying side by side, cop and robber are one and the same: neither hero, nor villain. But, once again, expressing a desire for postwar resurrection, the camera looks up and sees in the distance a group of school children on a hike, singing in the sun for the first time after a long winter.

Ikiru (*To Live,* 1952, shown in America in 1960) is a further variation on Kurosawa's theme of compassion and hope. A petty government official learns he is dying of cancer and, for the first time in his life, realizes that he has accomplished nothing. His reaction is to have a good time; he takes all his savings and spends them in a long, wild evening. But this proves disappointing. In one scene, drunk to the world and cold sober within, he sings, tears running down his cheeks, a faded little song he remembers from childhood. Before he dies, the clerk uses all his strength to implement a petition that has been lying for months on his desk and on the desks of others—a request for a park. In the teeth of

The plot of **Throne of Blood** *comes almost intact from* **Macbeth**, *but Kurosawa removed Shakespeare's ambitious Scottish thane to a medieval Japanese landscape. Below, the oriental Macbeth, played by Toshiro Mifune, leads an assault on a hill fortress.*

THRONE OF BLOOD (1957)

official indifference and antagonism, he pushes his project through. Finally it is complete and that night, sitting on a swing in the park, with the snow falling around him, he dies. *Ikiru*, as sweeping an indictment of bureaucracy as has ever been filmed, is not an angry motion picture. Kurosawa is not concerned with a bad society so much as with a good man— a flawed, less-than-ideal, but good human being.

Of all the films Kurosawa has made, *Seven Samurai*, or *The Magnificent Seven* (*Shichinin-no Samurai*, 1954, shown in a cut version in America in 1956), is generally considered his masterpiece. Bandits are about to attack a small village; the villagers seek the aid of a group of masterless samurai, men as outside society as the robbers they are asked to fight. The samurai agree; they win; and a number of them die. The villagers are grateful, but it is spring planting season, and they have work to do. The remaining samurai leave the village they have defended.

It is only toward the end of the film that the two sides, samurai and bandits, engage in combat. And then, where most films would have ended—a battle and the victory for the right side being judged enough—Kurosawa begins. The screen darkens, as though a chapter had ended, and in a lyrical sequence the villagers emerge for the first time as the figures of importance. It becomes apparent then that the samurai were fighting only for themselves, fighting for an ideal that those of them who survive come to understand as hollow. In the final scene the camera raises to the burial mounds, and the leader of the samurai says, "We have lost . . ." (there are no victors in war). Samurai and bandits are one, equally defeated; but the villagers, the enduring people of the world, oblivious of the "brave" deeds, will go on planting new rice. *The Magnificent Seven* cost more money than any previous Toho movie, took more than a year to complete, and had (in the uncut version) a running time of just under three hours. The film remains Kurosawa's strongest statement of the moral theme common to all his films: that human frailty must be accepted; but not passively, for man may overcome adversity and achieve his own salvation. All the contradictions embedded in Kurosawa's cinematic philosophy are brought together here, and the very tensions between them give the film its great strength.

There has been a looping back to earlier themes in Kurosawa's more recent films, *Yojimbo* and *Sanjuro Tsubake*, which revert to the satire of, for example, his *Those Who Tread on the Tiger's Tail*, made in 1945. *Yojimbo* (not yet shown in America) won a Venice Festival prize in 1961.

In this hilarious lampoon of empty heroics, Toshiro Mifune (an actor who appears in many of Kurosawa's films) comes to town in time to stop a war between rival families. The families have disguised all their ruling passions—greed, hate, malice—as "noble determination" and "pride." Only Mifune, like the little boy who sees that the emperor has no clothes, realizes the truth and succeeds in exposing the sham heroism at the end. More incisive, and even funnier, is

THE LOWER DEPTHS (1957)

In transplanting a band of beggars from the Russian hovel of Maxim Gorky's play to the Japanese cellar of his film, Kurosawa succeeded in recapturing both the bleak agony of The Lower Depths *and its elated moments—as in the song-and-dance below.*

Sanjuro Tsubake (made in 1962 and also not yet shown in America), which might be considered a sequel to *Yojimbo*. Nine young samurai are on a mission of revenge. They are filled with the usual intensity of spirit, self-importance, involvement, and dedication—until they meet a masterless samurai (again played by Mifune) who takes them thoroughly apart. At the same time, the samurai helps the young men and teaches them. At the start, when the grateful youngsters all bow low and say they do not know how they can ever repay him, his casual suggestion that they try money is totally disillusioning to them. Here Kurosawa is firmly explaining that the real samurai is someone who, no less human than others, simply tries harder.

These recent films show Kurosawa at his best, his style and statement complementing and reinforcing each other to produce a genuine work of cinematic art. He is not, of course, infallible. The most frequently repeated criticism of his work is that it is marred by an "infatuation with the look of his own image," and thus suffers from "dragginess." He has also been criticized for achieving "triteness" instead of the profound compassion that he admires in Dostoevsky; for excessive introspection, even narcissism; for permitting his style to obscure his statement, producing elaborate works of photographic beauty that amount to so much stylistic gymnasticism. And one critic found, even in his first film, "too many hidden implications."

This sort of criticism derives not so much from Kurosawa's concern for technique as from his philosophy, and from a failure on the part of his critics to understand it. Far from having broken with Japanese tradition, he has made its uniquely Japanese quality understandable and meaningful. His formality—in film structure, in acting style—is the formality of Japanese art, as in the *haiku* or in the classical theatre. His preoccupation with technique is completely Japanese; it is what one sees in the potter or carpenter, those other Japanese professions in which simple craftsmen may achieve a style. His obscurities are also those implicit in Japanese thought, in the classical Japanese conflict between duty and inclination. Kurosawa is at the same time so individualistic that many Japanese critics find him "Western." He does not subscribe to the Japanese myth of human (which is to say, Japanese) infallibility, the preference for demigods over men. For Kurosawa the "merely human" is quite enough, even if it leads him into his not-quite-convincing reliance on the message of hope. Action may define and save a man (in Japan as elsewhere), but if truth is merely relative, mere hope is not enough. It is perhaps this dilemma in Kurosawa, precisely this tension, that makes his films meaningful and provocative in both his world and ours.

Donald Richie, author of several books on Japan and its movies, including The Japanese Film *(Grove Press), designed the Kurosawa Retrospective at the Berlin Film Festival and is now editing* Three Screenplays of Akira Kurosawa.

Comedy has enlivened most of Kurosawa's movies, but recently he has made a number of outright satires, including Yojimbo, *in which the bemused-looking aristocrats (below) become aware that a long-standing feud between two clans has been pointless.*

YOJIMBO (1960)

TOHO INTERNATIONAL, INC.

On Stage: ZOHRA LAMPERT

Zohra Lampert is romping through what is easily the most unlikely theatrical career in recent history. In the past year she has been in two monumentally unsuccessful Broadway plays (*Look: We've Come Through*, which ran for five nights, and *First Love*, which ran a total of three weeks) and two remarkably undistinguished films. But, in spite of this inauspicious record, she is one of the most sought-after young actresses in New York; and recently—an impressive tribute to an actress in her twenties—she was awarded the supreme accolade: a play is being written specially for her.

Miss Lampert's "presence," the quality that has seen her through these star-crossed enterprises, is one of a quietly inept creature who believes in some great, secret love: the first aspect hilarious; the second, engaging. Whether talking about Picasso and Kafka over breakfast or doing the twist with a puppy in her pocket (as she did in one of her films), Miss Lampert is at once entrancing and jarringly comic. Indeed, if a clown wears both the tragic and comic masks at the same time, and evokes both tears and laughter with a single pratfall, then Zohra Lampert is one of those exceedingly rare creatures, a female clown.

Miss Lampert is not, in any conventional sense, a glamourous young woman. Yet, both on stage and off, she does manage to construct a sort of glamour, a warmth that might even be described as a radiance, from most unlikely attributes: she moves awkwardly, is tense and tight-lipped in her speech, gestures from the joints in her elbows rather like a marionette, and frequently looks (though, decidedly, she is not) almost cross-eyed. In a review of her performance in *Maybe Tuesday* (which ran on Broadway for five performances during 1958) Walter Kerr relished Miss Lampert's "froggy voice" and "blinding lack of intelligence"; and, he concluded, "the whole effect is charming."

The only child of Russian immigrants, and the niece of the late Argentinian Yiddish actor Samuel Iris, Zohra Lampert grew up in New York, attended the High School of Music and Art, and in a breezy two and half years received her B.A. degree from the University of Chicago. Her first professional theatrical experience was with the Playwrights company in Chicago where, under the direction of Paul Sills, she worked in a troupe that included Mike Nichols, Barbara Harris, and Gene Troobnick, performing in plays by Brecht, Büchner, Pirandello, Sophocles, and Kafka. (Her fondness for such plays has caused her to forsake Broadway at times and return to Chicago during the summer to work with Sills at The Second City and Playwrights.) Six years ago, after a short stint with the Chicago group, Miss Lampert came to New York and, with the grand goal of becoming an artist in mind, began studying with the acting coach Mira Rostova.

Since coming to New York, she has been in several films (they include *Pay or Die* with Ernest Borgnine, *Splendor in the Grass* with Warren Beatty, and *Hey, Let's Twist* with Joey Dee and the Starlighters), has made several off-Broadway appearances, and flashed past quickly on a number of television screens and almost as quickly in those Broadway disasters. However Miss Lampert's ill-fated vehicles have not succeeded in jinxing her. In fact they have served most often to show the extraordinary ability she has to turn mediocre and bad characterizations into engrossing, even brilliant, performances. She now lives by herself on Manhattan's East Side, in an apartment partly furnished with old set pieces from her plays, and spends most of her time reading scripts. She has rejected more than half a dozen since *First Love*, with the explanation: "I want to play something that has some substance. Whether the classics or Pinter or Ionesco, it doesn't matter. But that's why I go back to Chicago, just to play roles that have some nobility, some intelligence."

Miss Lampert's desire to perform in roles of "substance" is perhaps grounded in a belief that if she can do well in poor roles, she can do even better in good ones. This premise finds support in at least one of her films. In *Splendor in the Grass* she portrays a waitress in the New Haven pizza joint where she meets Yale-man Warren Beatty. Shortly after they meet, the two find themselves married and living on a farm, with one child on the kitchen floor and another child on the way. Beatty's former love, attractively played by Natalie Wood, visits the farm. She enters the kitchen where Zohra Lampert is leaning, perspiring, over a greasy stove, pats the baby on the head, and leaves. When Beatty escorts the girl out of the room, the sole tender moment in the movie occurs: Miss Lampert looks down at her singularly unattractive pregnancy, her dirty blue dress, and shrugs. A foolish, unco-ordinated shrug, one of simple acceptance. And in that gesture is all the glamour the character never had, all the hours in the squalid kitchen on the squalid farm, all the humdrum of the past twenty and next forty years of her life, and all her compassion and love for her husband and children. If the film script is not an inspired piece of writing, Zohra Lampert—at least for the few moments while she is on the screen—makes it seem inspired.

This then is Miss Lampert's special attraction. She may be first and most simply a comic, but underlying the comic quality is a sense of pathos and tenderness that indicates the genuine talent of an actress; and it is this added dimension that makes Zohra Lampert unique.

CHARLES L. MEE, JR.

ograph by PETER BASCH

In Print: JANE JACOBS

Sooner or later, in any discussion of the American City today, the name of Jane Jacobs is bound to be mentioned. The reason is not far to seek. Last year a book was published challenging, in fact totally reversing, the assumptions on which orthodox city planning had so far been based. During the same year a group of private citizens in New York City—with a hitherto unbeatable alliance of public officials and real-estate speculators arrayed against them—fought to a standstill and ultimately defeated the so-called "redevelopment" of their own neighborhood. Both the book and the battle, as it happens, owe most to the efforts of Mrs. Jacobs, a Greenwich Village housewife and architectural-magazine editor. She was chairman of the Save-the-West-Village campaign, and ran it straight out of the book—and she wrote the book.

If the lawyer's idea of aroused civic conscience is a runaway jury, then Jane Jacobs is the amateur's equivalent: a one-woman, runaway P.T.A. meeting. Last October, when the City Planning Commission held a hearing at City Hall to announce that Mrs. Jacobs' neighborhood had been designated a "blighted" area, suitable for urban renewal, she and her fellow Villagers rose from the audience in such a manifestation of community wrath that police had to be called to clear the room. As a result, she has acquired a reputation among city planners as a sort of Madame Defarge leading an aroused populace to the barricades, an impression she naturally disclaims. "There seems to be a notion that I run these people," she has said. "But I wouldn't have dreamed of telling them how to behave. I wouldn't have been chairman next week if I had. I was an instrument of what the neighborhood wanted to do."

Mrs. Jacobs wants her neighborhood improved, but she likes it fine. One of the best portions of her book, *The Death and Life of Great American Cities,* is a description of how life goes forward on the street in front of her house—its comings and goings, the ways in which civic discipline is threatened and maintained, a "ballet" of lively urban existence. She brings to city life, in contrast to most writers on the subject, some of the same warmth and curiosity that has long been lavished on the small country town. "Thornton Wilder's loving portrait of the leisurely life of Grover's Corners," as Brooks Atkinson remarks, "is no more romantic than Mrs. Jacobs' affectionate portrait of a day and night in Hudson Street."

She believes in the city's vitality and variety, the presence of people in motion, the disorders and diversities that make a great city delightful to those who love it, infuriating to those who want to reorganize it. She has inhabited and marveled at New York since she came from Scranton, Pennsylvania, in the early 1930's, and she practices her urban principles. The house on Hudson Street where she and her architect-husband live with their three children is situated between a laundry and a tailor shop. Nearby are tenements, modern apartment buildings, and here and there a deserted structure whose windows bear the telltale white X of demolition to come (see photograph). This is a "low-rental" area, but what Jane Jacobs has managed to prove—both to many readers of her book and to the city government—is that it is not a slum.

For the clearing of slums, and their replacement with aseptic modern structures, is no longer the liberal's utopian objective that it once was. Urban renewal, beginning as a banner of enlightenment, has become a watchword for a mixture of destructiveness and exploitation, mildly flavored with profiteering. There has come into being a mixture of legal provisions and tax allowances that, in sum, make it profitable to tear down nearly any building and replace it with a worse one. What happens, when communities are not watchful, is that a speculative builder may concoct a project to suit his own convenience and then get the municipal authorities to declare an area "blighted" so that he can carry it out. The result is a tax-supported raid on the city's social and human resources.

"These real-estate grabbers," says Mrs. Jacobs. "You'd think there was oil under the ground here." She is wise in the ways of local politics, which is one of the reasons she and her associates won; they knew what their enemies were up to, and their intelligence-net was effective. Once she found out about a plan for street-widening (for which read: sidewalk-narrowing) when her children told her about it. (The next time they spoke to workmen in the street they were told: "We don't talk to no little kids.") If she is criticized, it is mostly for being harsh with planners, who are not always quite the villains she makes them out. What she is fighting, as Herbert Gans wrote of her in *Commentary*, is not so much a doctrine as a way of life. What the American Middle Class wants—suburbs, throughways, shopping centers—is not what Mrs. Jacobs wants to see downtown, not what (in her view) makes a city work.

Her originality is only beginning to be felt, and even critics of her book concede that it has permanently changed the climate of debate about the City. When the West Village victory was finally announced, she issued a statement saying that "our sympathy goes out to other areas," which must have caused shivers in some quarters. Another contest would find her ready. "One thing I liked about this fight," she says, gesturing toward a paper-filled carton in the corner of her dining room; "We won it without a filing system. Everything we needed was always near the top."

ERIC LARRABEE

Photograph by RUTH O

Not far from its Burgundian source, the infant Seine meanders through the village of Billy

From source to estuary, the Seine lavishes her curves and geniality upon those drawn to her—and who is not? Artists endlessly pursue her image, each finding his own: the camera complements the sight of the brush

THE WELL-LOVED RIVER

By PIERRE SCHNEIDER   *Photographs by* HENRI CARTIER-BRESSON

The prestige of "the glorious river Seine," as Anatole France called her, is almost incomprehensibly disproportionate to her length: a mere rivulet when compared to the Amazon, the Nile, or the Danube. And yet, to those who know her, she—let us call her she, being all curves and, besides, the daughter of Bacchus— is the very paragon of rivers. When Dr. François Bernier reached the banks of the Ganges in 1665, on his way to the court of the Great Mogul to act as the latter's private physician, he "seemed," according to his companion Tavernier, "much surprised to find that the Ganges was no wider than the Seine in front of the Louvre." In that case, why go? The French are notoriously allergic to emigration. "We don't have Venice and its moon, nor its breeze, nor its lagoon, but we have the Seine," sang Parisian canoeists a century ago. Some people apparently did not even suspect the existence of other rivers. When Mme Grand, passing through Lyon, was shown the Saône, she exclaimed: "The Saône! Oh, how differently it is pronounced from Paris. In Neuilly we say 'the Seine!'" In a sense the frivolous lady was right, for

through the centuries Paris has been the center of France, and Paris owes its predominance to the Seine. For what made the rulers of the Ile-de-France, initially just a small medieval fief, prevail in the end over other, often stronger feudal lords, was the key position they occupied on the river. Thus her course is not so short after all: she runs through 500 miles of French countryside and twenty centuries of French history and civilization.

The way she runs provided her with her name and another key to the mystery of her importance. "Seine" comes from *Sequana*, which in turn is a latinized version of the Celtic word *skwan*, meaning "winding." In a straight line, the distance between spring and estuary is only 250 miles—just about half that of her actual itinerary. No other river shows such reluctance to reach the sea, and quite understandably: from Burgundy to Normandy she traverses some of France's most exquisite landscapes. In Paris she behaves like the American student who comes to visit, is conquered, and finds a pretext to stay: it is not until she has meandered three times through the city that she consents to move on.

In its upper reaches the Seine is strictly pour la pêche . . .

Geologists, of course, have another explanation. Between spring and estuary, the difference in altitude is a paltry 1,500 feet, a fact that prevents her from rushing headlong to her end. Then too, the low quota of clay in her bed enables it to absorb sudden increases in the flow of water. Dramatic floods have occurred, but they are few and far between. Elderly Parisians still remember the winter of 1910 when several quarters were inundated. The worst flood took place in 1176. Bridges, houses, cattle, everything was carried away, until the Bishop of Paris accompanied by the king and his court, came to the river and showed her the nail that had been used to pierce Christ's hand, saying "May this sign of the Holy Passion return thy waters to their bed and protect this unhappy people!" They did. Our godless age has constructed dams and built up the banks. Anyway, it should be said that whatever floods occur are not the fault of the Seine but of her more torrentuous tributaries, the Marne and the Yonne: When you throw a big party, how can you prevent a few obnoxious strangers from crashing it?

On the whole, however, the Seine is smooth and slow. The virtue of that slowness has deeply impressed itself on the French spirit—how deeply can be sensed if we remember that the Seine's course is literally a demonstration of how a little can be made to go a long way. French vocabulary is extremely limited when compared to English, but every word is made to bear a maximum weight. Racine's tragedies seem narrow next to Shakespeare's, but they compensate in intensity for what they lack in extensiveness. A few apples, a small mountain, and some pine-covered rocks were all that Cézanne needed to revolutionize modern painting. An analysis of the mainstream of French culture must lead to the conclusion that its behavior parallels that of the Seine.

. . . but at Mussy-sur-Seine, on its way toward Troyes, it becomes the village laundry

In reaching that conclusion so quickly, however, I have shown myself most disrespectful toward her message. So let me start again. But where? The answers seems simple: at the beginning. Unfortunately, the Seine has several. Is its source at Mount Tasselot, or near Saint-Seine l'Abbaye, or elsewhere? Specialists have long argued about it. The dilemma was finally bypassed, if not solved, when Napoleon III's government ordered the construction of a monument at the spring gushing near Saint-Seine. It is a fake grotto, with a basin, above which reclines a grotesquely academic female figure in stone. The responsible authorities have committed a twofold sin: against taste by perpetrating such a horror, and against truth by leading us to believe that greatness is a birthmark. Actually, nothing distinguishes this thin trickle of water from its numerous brothers in the neighborhood.

For the Seine's origins, we also have a choice between two legends. The pagan one relates how the nymph Sequana, relaxing on a Channel beach (no doubt the future site of Deauville), was espied and pursued by Neptune; she fled inland and, as her lecherous tormentor was about to catch her, implored the gods' help. They turned her into water and, much against his wish, Neptune had to wash his hands of her. In fact, this myth transcribes a natural phenomenon still observed today: the Seine's estuary is so broad that the sea's tide moves up along it, occasionally throwing up on the forefront of its progress a fierce-looking band of waves known as the *barre*, or the *mascaret*. The Christian legend, on the other hand, tells how the aged Saint Seine, returning one evening to the abbey he had founded, saw his donkey kneel down to make it easier for him to dismount and, more miraculous still, saw a spring welling up at the spot where the animal had kneeled. Different as the two stories are, they agree on one point: the curative virtues of the spring. Archaeological evidence, interpreted by medical authorities, shows that immersion in, or absorption of, Seine water was particularly effective against eye sores, sterility, imbecility, venereal disease, cellulitis, and hermaphroditism.

A few paces away from this spot a plank has been thrown across the rill; far downstream, at Tancarville, the Seine is spanned by a bridge nearly one mile long—the longest in Europe. Still, that plank deserves a pause: since civilizations grew up on the banks of rivers, bridges must have been one of man's earliest and most precious inventions. The last war, which destroyed so many of them, showed us how thoroughly their collapse short-circuits the current of community life. I do not know how many bridges there are on the Seine (more than thirty in Paris alone), but I do know that no public buildings are as deeply imprinted in the affections of Parisians. The earliest, the Petit Pont, has been destroyed and rebuilt sixteen times during the past thousand years. The Pont Neuf—which, by a quirk of history, is now the oldest surviving bridge—was the first not to be lined with houses and the first public thoroughfare to sport sidewalks. It quickly became an open-air salon where mountebanks, quacks, and barbers performed, watched by crowds of *flâneurs*; hence the saying, "At any time, on the Pont Neuf, you are sure to meet a monk, a white horse, and a whore." For a while it lost its role as Paris's promenade deck to the Pont des Arts, built by Napoleon Bonaparte on his return from Egypt. He lined it with orange and pomegranate trees, and with benches in the Roman style. Gone today are the fig and orange trees; gone, in fact, is Bonaparte's Pont des Arts; but on the present "temporary" bridge—in France temporary has a way of meaning permanent— the city's last organ grinder still performs.

The Pont Neuf's first stone was laid by King Henri III; the Pont de la Concorde, on the other hand, close by the spot where Louis XVI was beheaded, was built with stones from the Bastille, whose destruction ushered in the fall of royalty. But bridges are more essential than those who cross them. After Napoleon's defeat at Waterloo, the king of Prussia wished to blow up the Pont d'Iéna, named after one of his most resounding disasters. Upon hearing this, Louis XVIII, though Napoleon's lifetime enemy, had himself wheeled onto the bridge and declared: "They shall have to blow us up together." The bridge still exists but arouses no interest, whereas the Pont de l'Alma, though no more handsome, does—at least at times when the Seine is rising. Then every Parisian comes to inspect how far the water has mounted along the leggings of the Zouave, a statue on one of the bridge's piers. On the bridge's other pier another stone soldier stands frozen at attention, a no less convenient flood barometer—but no one has ever been concerned with him.

That kind of apparent injustice is quite in keeping with the Seine's character. When, at Marcilly, she meets her first important tributary, the Aube, the latter is the bigger of the two streams. Yet the Seine's name prevails. At this early stage the Seine is so inconspicuous as to be almost invisible, except from a bridge. You can tell her meandering course only by the trees that crowd her banks. Among them, poplars dominate, as they do along so many French roads. But then, Pascal has pointed out that "rivers are walking roads that carry us where we wish to go." Napoleon phrased this thought more matter-of-factly: "Paris, Rouen, Le Havre, are all one city of which the Seine is the main street." Nature invented the conveyor belt. Indeed, rivers are the world's earliest instance of automation, though it took men a long time to realize it: the earliest wills date back to the time of Augustus. It took man far less time to discover another use of the river: as washing machine. The Seine's early course is lined with countless *lavoirs,* where kneeling women clean the family linens and blemish their neighbors' reputations. As we move downstream, the washhouses disappear under the double impact of household appliances and pollution.

A different sort of pollution is first encountered near Anglure on the Aube: world history. The town's lord had been captured by Saladin during the Third Crusade. He had been allowed to return home on his word of honor in order to collect the money for his ransom and, having failed, he went back into captivity. Touched by such honesty, Saladin set him free on the condition that all the lords of Anglure were henceforth to bear Saladin as their (un)Christian name and that he build two mosques in his domains. One still exists at tiny Clesles on the Marne, but is now called the Fromage Tower, after the cheeses stored in it. The hostility to the exotic evident in this coarse anticlimax is a fundamental characteristic of the French spirit: the classic poet Boileau ends his enchanting description of the Seine at Haute-Isle, his rustic retreat, with this rather unexpected couplet:

Its banks are lined with willows planted by nature
And with nut trees oft insulted by the passer-by.

It is my contention that the French invented the *vespasienne* to make it perfectly clear that this kind of insult is not the consequence of a pressing need but a gesture freely willed: a deliberate affront to sublimity. Restif de la Bretonne left another such footnote scratched into a parapet on the Ile Saint-Louis, Paris's loveliest island. Commenting on an enchanting love affair, he wrote: "She made me happy, I made her pregnant, we are even."

With the absorption of the Yonne at Montereau, the Seine reaches adulthood, an age she inaugurates in the same manner

The upper Seine grows by many tributaries. One of these, entering at Melun, is the subject of Paul Cézanne's Bridge at Maincy *(1879). This was for him a rare venture into impressionist territory: almost alone among the great French painters of his time, Cézanne remained for the most part unmoved by the Seine and its shimmering light.*

57

"Every picture," said Alfred Sisley, "shows a spot with which the artist has fallen in love." In his Nut Trees at Thomery, *painted in 1880, the spot he has so obviously fallen in love with is a gentle stretch of the widening Seine near the edge of the Forest of Fontainebleau, and the trees are very likely some of its famous chestnuts.*

as humans: with military service. At Montereau, Napoleon won his last big battle. The dangerously genial Emperor is a splendid illustration of how closely the course of French history is entwined with that of the Seine: he abdicated at Fontainebleau and lived stormy days with Josephine at Malmaison; his first action after arriving in Paris—by riverboat—as a hungry Corsican youth was to browse along the quays; and had Europe's monarchs known the title of the battered book he purchased, well might they have trembled—it was *Gil Blas,* the story of a poor but ambitious boy who rose to absolute power. In his will Napoleon wrote: "I desire my ashes to rest on the banks of the Seine, amid the French people whom I loved so much." In 1840 the French government asked Great Britain for permission to make the transfer from Saint Helena. Lord Palmerston agreed to the request, though he thought it "very French." No record survives to show whether the throwing of Joan of Arc's ashes into the Seine at Rouen was regarded by the Dauphin as very English. Be that as it may, Napoleon's remains traveled solemnly up the Seine that year, to a great display of popular emotion, aboard the *Dorade III,* one of the steamships with the huge wheels and beanstalk chimneys introduced on the Rouen-Paris route only a short time before. Forty years earlier a certain Mr. Fulton, an American, had sought to interest Napoleon in an invention with which he was experimenting on the Seine, "a water-chariot moved by fire," as a contemporary described it. "Impostor," had been the Emperor's curt reply.

Its eminent navigability was of course the Seine's chief quality from the outset. The Gauls had sailed and rowed on her and floated logs down her course; she was particularly precious in those troubled centuries when roads were few, bad, and dangerous. Even today, however, the traffic is intense. Rouen is 80 miles away from the sea, yet its importance as a port is equal to that of Le Havre; and cargo ships push as far inland as Paris, whose port, in terms of tonnage, is among the largest in France. Still, they are intruders, like the sea gulls whose squeals are heard on certain days along the quays, or like the speedboats used by newspapers to deliver their latest editions more swiftly than the traffic-jammed streets would allow. Far truer to Sequanian style were the old river-coaches; distances were short, but the sluggish pace of these forerunners of the *bateaux-mouches* seemed like a real cruise. And, as on cruises, poignant idyls blossomed: the hero and heroine of Flaubert's *Education sentimentale* meet on the ship that carried Napoleon's ashes, and Alain-Fournier made on a *bateau-mouche* the brief, hopeless encounter that was to inspire the most romantic scene of *Le Grand Meaulnes.* But really to understand the river's mentality and rhythm, we must turn to those surviving monsters of a less hectic age: the barges.

From north, east, west, and south, along tributaries and canals, they come puttering and creeping (towage by humans has disappeared, and the use of horses is on its way to extinction). It takes great strength of character to accept the excruciating slowness of barge life: barge people are a race apart, and the gap between them and landlubbers widens, if anything, as the tempo on the firm ground becomes faster and faster. Barge children feel uprooted when they are sent to school on land. Cases of landlubbers becoming successful bargemen are almost unknown, and few girls who marry a bargeman can bear fluvial life more than three or four years. Until recently, many river people could neither read nor write. Legislation has only lately ceased to treat them as nomads. They are wary of terra firma, venture on it only at certain bridgeheads, drink at their own *bistros,* shop at their own grocery stores (usually run by lockkeepers), and whenever possible, as at Conflans-Sainte-Honorine, pray in their own church— a barge, naturally. Between them and earth, the distance is but a few steps, yet they are worlds away, too busy holding the wheel and forging ahead to step ashore: a five-minute pause may mean a three-hour delay at the next lock.

Infinite patience, detachment, and preservation of customs that hark back to a quieter, saner universe—a universe still in touch with its wellsprings—are the presents the river lavishes upon those who approach her closely. Nowhere is the contrast more striking than in the heart of frantic Paris. To step down from the busy, car-jammed avenues along the Seine to the waterside quays is to regress into the past. Down here, grass grows between uneven cobblestones, poplars mirror themselves in the lazy current, the noise above is reduced to an agreeable hum. Whoever walks here is engaged in timeless activities: lovers embracing, old men chatting, a master walking his dog. The Seine is the natural ally of those who, temporarily or forever, have rejected the bonds of society: *clochards,* painters, and fishermen. One of the heartening things about Paris is to see how many fishermen are left in it and the fascinated attention with which their quixotic efforts are followed by passers-by.

They are still exactly as Daumier sketched them. "Oh woe!" exclaims a rain-soaked lady shivering beside her husband who clings stoically to his rod, "Oh to have dreamt all my maiden years of a spouse who would share my taste for poetry, and to hit upon a husband who only likes minnows!" A poet he may not be, but a philosopher he is beyond doubt. "The fisherman," Daumier himself comments elsewhere, "is the truly independent, persevering, and resigned man; adversity does not discourage him." Indeed, I suspect him of being almost disappointed when he catches a fish: he is not doing it for profit.

In Draveil, just above Paris, children come down to the Seine for a festival . . .

At street level the browser is the intellectual equivalent of the fisherman down below. No less superbly indifferent to passing time and to social pressure, he plunges his eyes into the oblong green boxes of the *bouquinistes*, hoping to hook a rare and useless masterpiece amid the piles of dusty books. This affinity between words and rivers is the profound reason for their proximity in Paris where, as Guillaume Apollinaire nicely wrote, "the Seine flows between banks of books." The spectacle of so completely harmonious a conjuncture between the physical and the spiritual is one of the most satisfactory to be encountered in our world. Few French writers have remained unreceptive to it. "The air that comes to me from the river is lighter than elsewhere," wrote the poet Léon-Paul Fargue, who also claims a *clochard* assured him he slept on the quais facing the Louvre because he dreamt more distinguished dreams there. Anatole France would certainly have agreed: "Inasmuch as there are trees there," he wrote, "with books, and as women pass there, it is the most beautiful place in the world."

The quays are one of the points where the Seine's influence on French ways of thinking and literature is most deeply felt. "By

frequenting those old, worm-eaten volumes," Anatole France remarked, "I gained, already as a child, a profound sense of the flowing away of things and of the universal nothingness." If that kind of wistful, resigned pessimism is so frequent in French literature, it is because of the Seine. Malherbe, Racine, La Rochefoucauld, Saint-Beuve, Baudelaire, and countless others owe it a great debt, which Guy de Maupassant acknowledged for them all when he wrote: "Ah! the beautiful, calm, varied, and stinking river, full of mirages and filth. I believe I loved her so much because she revealed to me the meaning of life."

With time the proportion of refuse augmented until, a century ago, Théophile Gautier scoffed:

> *The Seine, black sewer of streets,*
> *Loathsome river fed by gutters,*
> *Dirties my foot . . .*

Was it while gazing at it that Verlaine came upon his definition of water, "that impure liquid, a drop of which is enough to spoil the transparency of absinthe"? But it has proved an insufficient deterrent to Paris's half-dozen swimming establishments on the river. It is one of the best proofs of the Parisians' continuing faith in

. . . while in nearby Ivry they come down to watch their fathers at work

the pristine purity of their river—an obstinacy worthy of barge-men and fishermen—that they continue to jump into it by the thousands despite the fact that the proportion of filth to mirage is crushing. They do so without illusions. "Hey, old boy! Is the water good?" asks a character in a swimming establishment cari-catured by Daumier (who lived right above one). "Young whip-persnapper, if it were good, it wouldn't cost a mere twenty cen-times."

The bond between bargemen, bathers, fishermen, and browsers is obvious: a certain insulation from the follies of modern life. Now insularity is an attribute of islands; hence Parisians have a veritable cult for theirs. Paris's nucleus, after all, is the Ile de la Cité, and its most handsome district the Ile Saint-Louis. In the eyes of Parisians, every island must be a desert island or a Cythera, and so they have long treated those that stud the Seine in the downstream suburbs as a combination of both. Today, mills and shanty-towns have all but conquered them; but here and there a rustic *guinguette*—where you can eat fried fish, drink *un petit vin blanc,* and promise eternal love to passing acquaintances —hangs on heroically, sandwiched between two factories. And I

confess to being moved beyond words by the sordid tavern facing the Ile Robinson, now turned into a grim coal dump, which con-tinues to call itself with desperate bravura: "The Balcony on the Islands."

The supreme attraction of islands remains yet to be mentioned: to reach them you must take a boat. Rowing and sailing attained, between 1860 and 1910, a popularity difficult to imagine at pres-ent. Maupassant was speaking for several generations that wore sailor shirts, straw hats, and mustaches, or twirled bright um-brellas, when he reminisced: "How many funny things and funny girls I saw during the days I spent canoeing! . . . a life of strength and carelessness, of gaiety and poverty, of robust and boisterous merrymaking."

The little boats often carried women—light women, so as not to weight down unduly their frail hulls. But the fickle grisettes who trusted whatever was left of their virtue to the river should not be judged too harshly. Their lack of morals was more than compensated for by their warmheartedness and a disarming ab-sence of snobbishness. Victor Hugo relates a charming example of these Sequanian traits. The Duc d'Aumale, son of King Louis-

TEXT CONTINUED ON PAGE 64

At the very heart of Paris, between the two halves of the Pont Neuf,

e de la Cité rides the Seine like a ship tugging at her mooring lines

The Seine serves all kinds of art: a painter at the Pont de Solférino . . .

TEXT CONTINUED FROM PAGE 61
Philippe, was wont to walk home along the riverside from the camp where he was stationed as a captain. On the banks he met, day after day, a young girl, Adèle Protat, with whom he gradually began to flirt. One day, as she was canoeing on the Seine near Neuilly, she saw two young men bathing. "That's the Duc d'Aumale," the boatman told her. Adèle grew pale and said, "Bah!" And Victor Hugo concludes: "Next day, she no longer loved him. She had seen him naked, and she knew he was a prince." She would certainly have felt more at ease in the company of Maupassant: "A woman is something indispensable on a boat. Indispensable because she keeps mind and heart awake, because she stimulates, amuses, distracts, lends spice, and completes the scenery with a red umbrella gliding against the green banks."

The picture evoked by these lines has, I am sure, brought a name to every reader's lips: Auguste Renoir. This is no coincidence. The very same places favored by Maupassant—Argenteuil, Bezons, Bougival, Chatou, *guinguettes* like La Grenouillère, and restaurants like Fournaise—were frequented and painted by Monet, Renoir, Manet, Sisley, and Pissarro. What attracted them to the river? The passion of the time for boating, to be sure. Sisley and Renoir sailed all the way down to Le Havre. Monet, taking a cue from his master Daubigny, spent long months on a studio-boat (see page 72). They found both pleasure and inspiration in the gay life of the Seine. "I was perpetually at Fournaise's," Renoir recalled later. "There I found as many splendid girls to paint as I wanted. One wasn't reduced as today to follow a little model in the street for an hour, only to be called a dirty old man in the end."

. . . and a fashion photographer on the barges near the Quai de Bercy

But the Seine had something more important to offer them: impressionism. For some years, they had been trying to break out of the closed forms and the dark, compartmented colors prevailing around 1860. It was the Seine that furnished them the instruments: light and water. Under their twofold assault, forms were broken up into a myriad of brilliant reflections loosened by the tremulous atmosphere and reverberated across fluid surfaces. Stable facts gave way to fleeting "impressions." From his studio-boat Monet observed "the effects of light from one twilight to the other." He first studied the Seine at Bonnières in 1868; later he worked in the company of Renoir near Bougival; in 1871 he moved to Argenteuil; later to Vétheuil; finally, to Giverny, where he died, half a century later. Yet he continued to pursue those passing impressions on his pond strewn with water lilies, till he

dissolved all objects and wed sun and water so indistinguishably that his ultimate paintings have been hailed as prefigurations of today's nongeometric abstraction. Line is the daughter of the solid, as color is the daughter of the liquid element: by drawing the impressionists to her bosom, the Seine had converted modern French painting to the latter, were it at the expense of the former. Quite logically, Vlaminck and Derain first tried their Fauve fireworks at Chatou; quite logically, too, Bonnard in search of a lighter palette moved to Vernonnet.

From Paris onward, the Seine belongs to painting. (Not upstream, strangely enough.) But it should not be inferred that the impressionists were the first artists to discover her. Others had worked on her banks before, and her lesson had permeated their work, though not as overtly. Corot often sojourned at Mantes:

the moist tenderness and the prophetic lightness of his canvases are to be attributed to the Seine's influence. Farther down, at Les Andelys, Poussin was born and initiated into his art. True, he left his birthplace as a young man, never to return, but it is not excessive to recognize in his fondness for opulent verdure and for rivers an unconscious nostalgia for his native land. Flamboyant ornament ripples on Gothic structures in many places but nowhere as animatedly as at Rouen, where it comes as a response to the tireless play of light and shadow on the water. Finally, it is in Honfleur and Le Havre, the harbors on the Seine's estuary, that Jongkind and Boudin painted the delicate, fluid oils and water colors that made them impressionism's precursors. How much the medium of water color is attuned to estuary conditions is apparent if we remember that Raoul Dufy came from Le Havre.

We have been moving along rather fast, but that is not surprising: since Paris, the Seine has grown considerably larger and events ashore more difficult to discern. Since 1850, when causeways were built to stabilize the final stretch of the Seine's course, Rouen has become a real sea harbor. Until then the river had had a most indecent way of changing beds from time to time. Lillebonne, Harfleur, and to some extent Honfleur have thus been stranded in the course of centuries—a fate as humiliating for a harbor as for a singer to lose his voice. Even within the existing bed, it used to take a clever pilot to pick out the navigable channels from the maze of treacherous shoals. Becoming stuck on a shoal could be fatal, especially at spring tides, when the *barre* would topple over vessels like bowling pins. The most famous ship to have suffered this tragic fate was the *Télémaque*, which sank opposite Quilleboeuf in 1790. Soon the rumor went round that it contained a fabulous treasure, some eighty-five million gold francs, which Louis XVI was trying to smuggle over to England. Time and again, people tried to raise the *Télémaque*. The last attempt was made in 1842 by a British engineer, Mr. Taylor, who convinced a number of gullible Frenchmen to sink their money into the undertaking. Then one night Taylor disappeared, leaving even his thirty-five British workmen unpaid. "The idea was too heavy, and the chains were too light," someone commented.

The moral is, never procrastinate in an estuary. Let us heed it. Already, Le Havre is visible on the starboard side. The water beneath our bow tastes of salt. The Seine yields to sea—but not before giving us, as a send-off present, one of the most beautiful stories ever told in honor of mankind. One day, while hunting in the forest of Roumare, which spreads in one of the Seine's last sweeping bends before Rouen, Rollo, Duke of Normandy, hung his gold bracelet on the branch of an oak. Three years later the bracelet was found, still dangling from the same branch.

All ages climb Notre-Dame's north tower

Pierre Schneider ordinarily contemplates the Seine from the quays of Paris, but for this article he followed it all the way to the sea. He has written about the artists Joan Miró, Nicolas Poussin, and Pierre Bonnard in previous issues of HORIZON.

Henri Matisse's Glimpse of Notre-Dame in the Late Afternoon *is a glimpse from his fifth-floor window on the Quai Saint-Michel, where he was living in 1902. "A fine view," he said, "with Notre-Dame to the right, the Palais de Justice and the Préfecture on the left." He painted it several times in the Fauve style he was then using.*

Left: Camille Pissarro painted The Louvre Seen from the Pont-Neuf, Winter *in 1902. Too ill to work outdoors, as a critic recalls, "one saw him at the window trying—with complete success—to conjure up on canvas one of the loveliest views in Paris . . . all that remained to him of youth."*

Below: Paul Signac's Pont Louis-Philippe, *painted in 1884 when he was twenty-one, is a view from the Right Bank across to the Ile Saint-Louis and the houses of the Quai de Bourbon. Signac, an ardent Seine sailor, celebrated other enthusiasms by naming his first boat* Manet-Zola-Wagner.

COLLECTION MR. AND MRS. LUDWIG NEUGASS, N.Y.C.

Overleaf: When Auguste Renoir painted his Oarsmen at Chatou *in 1879, the little village just below Paris had not yet been engulfed in suburbs. The man in the foreground is Gustave Caillebotte, part-time painter, wealthy patron, and mentor to several impressionists in their boat-building schemes.*

69

71

Above: Claude Monet and Edouard Manet spent the summer of *1874* in Argenteuil, about six miles below Paris, where they both had boats and used them as floating studios. This little green barge (a detail from a somewhat larger canvas) is Manet's boat as painted by Monet—who, in turn, was painted at work in his boat by Manet.

Right: The Bridge at Mantes (*1868–70*) is a view by Camille Corot, who did not paint the river often but on this occasion made it the subject of one of his finest works. Mantes, some forty miles below Paris, has earned a place in history as well as art: William the Conqueror sacked the city in *1087* and was mortally wounded there.

The sentinel poplars at Mantes . . .

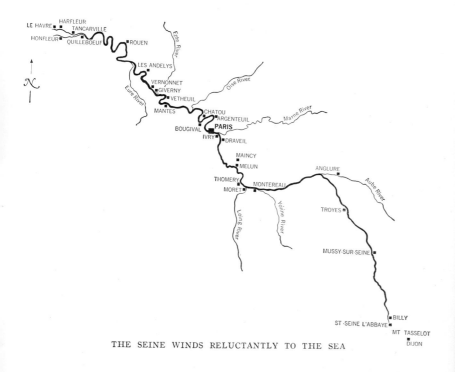

THE SEINE WINDS RELUCTANTLY TO THE SEA

. . give way at Rouen to factory stacks and the towers of the great cathedral

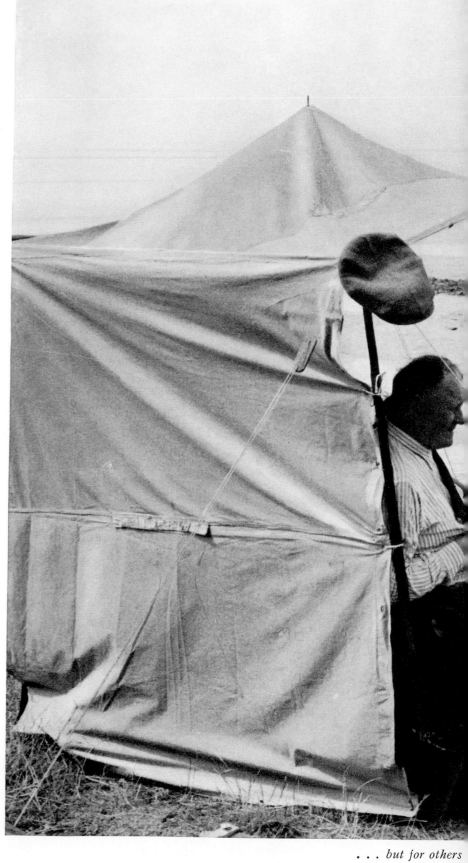

. . . but for others

For some, Honfleur means fishing . . .

eans a last chance to sit beside the Seine: beyond lies the English Channel

The Breakwater at Honfleur *(1864) was Claude Monet's first painting to attract real attention, bu*

got very little credit for it: the admiring public, misreading a vowel, thought it was by the then much better-known Manet

JEAN ROUBIER

Mankind, especially in the West, has long lived under its spell, and expressed in art and philosophy our brooding over Time's passage. But what if scientists could circumvent its hitherto unchanging pace?

THE

Man is the only animal to be troubled by Time, and from that concern comes much of his finest art, a great deal of his religion, and almost all his science. For it was the temporal regularity of nature—the rising of sun and stars, the slower rhythm of the seasons—that led to the concept of universal order and in turn to astronomy, the first of all sciences.

Time has been basic to all religions, where it has been combined with such ideas as reincarnation, foretelling the future, resurrection, and the worshiping of the heavenly bodies—as shown by the monolithic calendar of Stonehenge, the Zodiac from Dendera, and the time-markers of the Maya (see following pages). Some faiths (Christianity, for instance) have placed Creation and the beginning of Time at very recent dates, and have anticipated the end of the universe in the near future. Other religions, such as Hinduism, have looked back through enormous vistas of Time and forward to even greater ones. It was with some reluctance that Western astronomers realized that the East was right—that the age of the universe is to be measured in billions rather than millions of years, if it can be measured at all.

And it is only in the past fifty years that we have learned something about the nature of Time itself, and have even been able to influence its progress, though as yet by no more than millionths of a second. Ours is the first generation

The angel on the base of the south tower at Chartres (left) was a reminder to medieval man of Time's strict and implacable authority. "Down from your full sundial," as the modern poet Rainer Maria Rilke wrote of her, "glide the hours."

By ARTHUR C. CLARKE

TYRANNY OF TIME

since balance wheels and pendulums started oscillating to realize that Time is neither absolute nor inexorable, and that the tyranny of the clock may not last forever. Man's experience tells him that Time may appear to rush or to linger, each second slowly following the next, depending on our moods. Now a scientific view is beginning to reveal the same possibility that Time may be relative and malleable.

It is hard not to think of Time as an adversary, and in a sense all the achievements of human civilization are the trophies that man has won in his war against Time. The cave artists at Lascaux were the first to discover a way of sending not merely their bones but some at least of their thoughts and feelings into the future. The invention of poetry, perhaps as part of religious rituals, was the next advance. Bards and minstrels like Homer carried in their heads the only record of prehistory we possess, though until the invention of writing it was always liable to distortion or total loss. Writing—perhaps the most important single invention that mankind ever made or ever will make—changed all that; and with the invention of the printing press, the written word became virtually immortal.

Little more than a century ago writing and the visual arts were reinforced by the wonderful recording devices of the phonograph and the camera. With their arrival Time lost its absolute control over sound and sight. No other artifact created by the brain or the hand is as evocative as a photograph. It alone can take our senses back into the past, can make us feel—in joy or sadness—"*This* is how it really was, in such a place and at such a time." Moreover, the camera—especially the movie camera, when it

arrived some fifty years later—gave us the power not merely to recapture Time but to dissect and distort it. Sights too swift or too slow for the human eye to follow were suddenly made visible by high-speed and time-lapse photography. Anyone who has watched the vicious battle to the death between two vines, tearing at each other with hour-long slashes of their tendrils, can never again feel the same way about the vegetable kingdom. The movements of clouds, the splash of a raindrop, the passage of the seasons, the beat of a hummingbird's wings—before our century men could only guess at these things, or glimpse them merely as independent, unrelated snapshots. Now we can watch them with our own eyes and see them as an organic, connected whole.

Impressive though the achievements of the past hundred years have been, they are pitiful when we consider what we would *like* to do about Time if we had the power. Such ideas as observing the past, prolonging the present, or seeing the future are common and perhaps universal fantasies. Let us see if they must always be so.

It is worth remembering that actually we never see or experience anything *but* the past. The sounds you are hearing now come from a thousandth of a second back in time for every foot they have to travel to reach your ears. What is true of sound is also true of light, though on a scale almost exactly a million times shorter. When we look out into space, we can see events that occurred centuries or even millions of years ago.

This is a very limited kind of penetration into the past, however; and it offers no possibility of seeing into our *own* past. Nor can we hope, when we have reached the worlds of

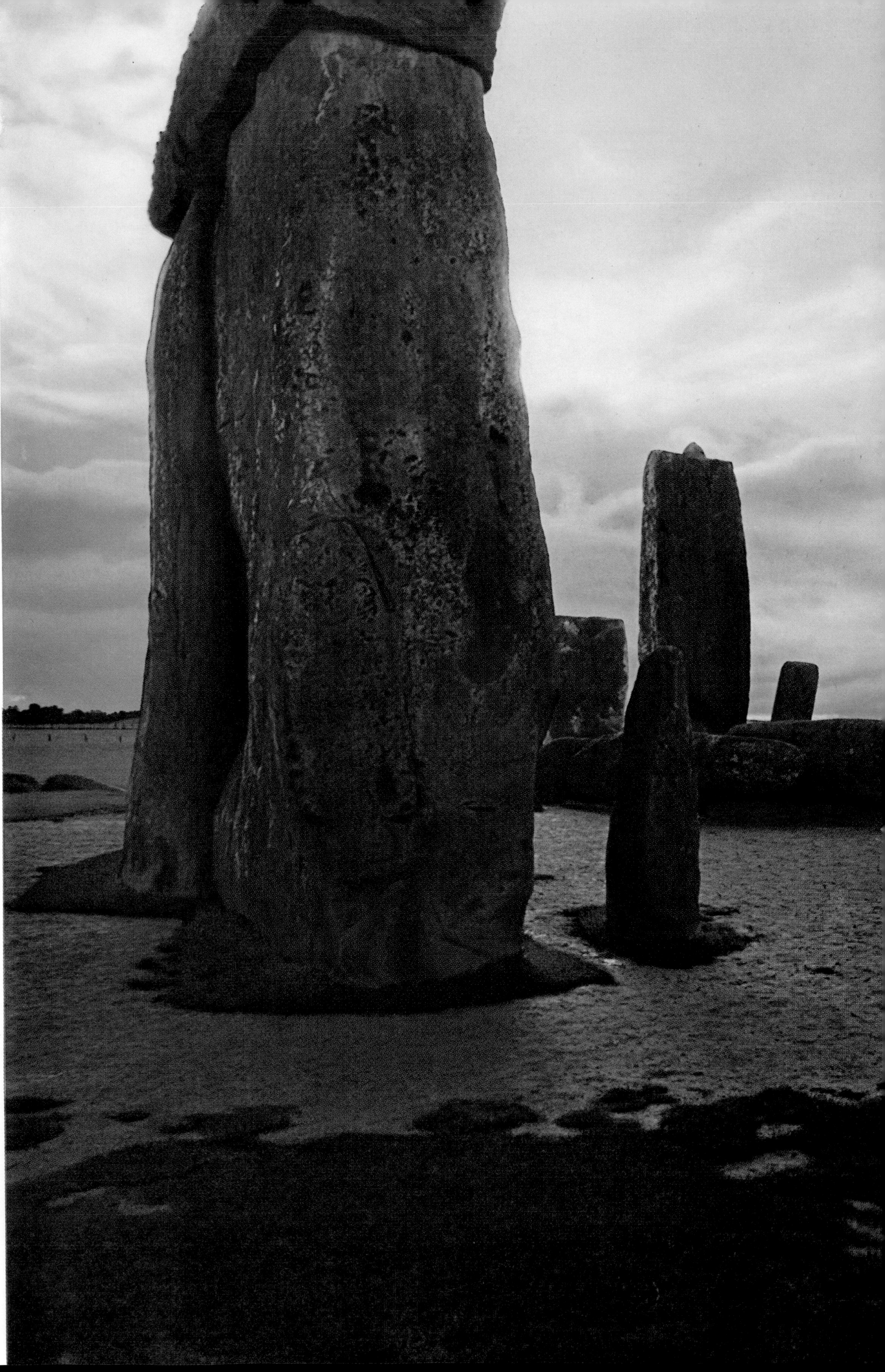

FRITZ HENLE–PHOTO RESEARCHERS

nearby suns, to find advanced races who have been watching us and recording our own lost history through supertelescopes—an idea that has been suggested by some science-fiction writers. The light waves from any events on the earth's surface are badly scrambled on their way out through the atmosphere—that is, if clouds allow them to escape at all. After that, they are so swiftly weakened by distance that no telescope could be built, even in theory, that would allow one to observe terrestrial objects smaller than several miles across, from the distance of Mars.

For there is a limit to the amplification of light, set by the nature of the light waves themselves, and no scientific advances can circumvent it. In much the same way we cannot hope to recapture vanished sounds, once they have dwindled below the general level of background noise. It has sometimes been said that no sound ever dies, but merely becomes too faint to be heard. This is not technically true: the vibrations from any sound are so swiftly damped out that within a few seconds they cease to exist in any physical sense. No amplifier can recapture the words that you spoke a minute ago; even if it had infinite sensitivity, it would merely reproduce the random hiss of the air molecules as they collide with one another. If there is any way in which we can ever observe the past, it must depend upon technologies not only unborn but today unimagined.

Yet the idea does not involve any logical contradictions or scientific absurdities, and in view of what has already happened in archaeological research, only a very foolish man would claim that it is impossible. We have now recovered knowledge from the past that it once seemed obvious must have been lost forever, beyond all hope of recovery. How could we possibly expect to measure the rainfall in the year A.D. 784? We now do it by examining the thickness of tree rings. How can we find the age of a piece of bone of unknown origin? Carbon 14 dating does just this. Which way did the compass needle point twenty thousand years ago? The orientation of magnetic particles in ancient clays will tell us. How has the temperature of the oceans varied during the past half million years? We now have—and this is perhaps the most amazing achievement of all—a "time thermometer," which follows the coming and going of the ice ages, so that we can say with some confidence that 210,000 years ago the average temperature of the sea was 84° F, whereas 30,000 years later it had dropped to 70°.

How has this been discovered? The trick is in knowing that the composition of the chalky shells of certain marine animals depends on the temperature of the water in which they were formed. From a delicate and sophisticated anal-

When our distant ancestors began to connect the changing seasons with the sun's progress around the sky, they built great calculators like Britain's Stonehenge (c. 1500 B.C.) where the rays of sunset and sunrise fall along a line between the huge monoliths at the summer and winter solstice.

ysis, Professor Harold Urey was thus able to tell that a fossil mollusk which lived in the seas covering Scotland 150 million years ago was born in the summer, when the water temperature was 70°, lived four years, and died in the spring.

Not long ago such knowledge of the past would have seemed clairvoyance, not science. It has been achieved through the development of sensitive measuring instruments (by-products, usually, of atomic research) that can detect the incredibly faint traces left upon objects by their past history. No one can yet say how far such techniques may be extended. There may be a sense in which all events leave some mark upon the universe, at a level not yet reached by our instruments (but possibly, in very abnormal circumstances, by our senses: Is this the explanation of ghosts?). The time may come when we can read such marks, now as invisible to us as the plain signs of a trail to an Indian scout or an aborigine tracker. And then the curtain will lift from the past.

At first sight, the ability to look back into Time would seem the most wonderful power that could be given to men. All lost knowledge would be recovered, all mysteries explained, all crimes solved, all hidden treasures found. History would no longer be a patchwork of surmises and conjectures; where today we guess, we would *know*. And perhaps we might even reach the stage so poetically described by H. G. Wells in his short story *The Grisly Folk:*

A day may come when these recovered memories may grow as vivid as if we in our own persons had been there and shared the thrill and fear of those primordial days; a day may come when the great beasts of the past will leap to life again in our imaginations, when we shall walk again in vanished scenes, stretch painted limbs we thought were dust, and feel again the sunshine of a million years ago.

With such powers we would be like gods, able to roam at will down the ages. But only gods, surely, are fit to possess such powers. If the past were suddenly opened up to our inspection, we would be overwhelmed not only by the sheer mass of material but by the brutality, horror, and tragedy of the centuries that lie behind us. It is one thing to read about massacres, battles, plagues, Inquisitions, or to see them enacted in the movies. But what man could bear to look upon the immutable evil of the past, knowing that what he saw was real and beyond all remedy? Better, indeed, that the good and the bad lie forever beyond such scrutiny.

And there is another aspect of the matter. How would *we* care for the idea that, at some unknown time in the future, men not unlike ourselves except for their superior science may be peering into our lives, watching all our follies and vices as well as our rarer virtues? The next moment that you are engaged in some discreditable action, pause to contemplate the thought that you may be a specimen before a class in primitive psychology a thousand years from now. A still worse possibility is that the voyeurs of some decadent future age may use their perverted science to spy upon our

To the ancient Egyptians the relativity of Time would have seemed quite natural. On the ceiling of the late Ptolemaic temple of Hathor at Dendera they incised a zodiac in which the signs we use today (inner circle) are surrounded by a division into thirty-six "decans" (outer circle) based on rising stars, combined with a civil and religious year of four units and a rural year of three: the July flooding of the Nile, the November plowing, and the March harvest.

lives. Yet perhaps even that is better than the prospect that we may be too simple and archaic to interest them at all.

To travel into the past, or to reach back through the ages and change events that have already occurred, involves so many paradoxes and contradictions that we are, surely, justified in regarding it as impossible. The classic argument against time travel is that it would allow a man to go back into the past and to kill one of his direct ancestors, thus making himself—and probably a considerable fraction of the human race—nonexistent.

Some ingenious writers have accepted this possibility and said, in effect: "Very well—suppose such paradoxes *do* occur. What then?" One of their answers is the concept of parallel time-tracks. They assume that the past is not immutable—that one could, for instance, go back to 1865 and deflect the aim of John Wilkes Booth in Ford's Theatre. But by so doing, one would abolish our world and create another, whose history would diverge so much from ours that it would eventually become wholly different.

Perhaps all possible universes have an existence, like the tracks in an infinite marshaling yard, but we merely move along one set of rails at a time. If we could travel backward and change some key event in the past, all that we would really be doing would be going back to a switch point and setting off on another time-track.

But it may not be as simple, if you will pardon the expression, as this. Other writers have developed the theme that even if we could change individual events in the past, the inertia of history is so enormous that it would make no difference. Thus you might save Lincoln from Booth's bullet, only to have another Confederate sympathizer waiting with a bomb in the foyer. And so on.

The most convincing argument against time travel is the remarkable scarcity of time travelers. However unpleasant our age may appear to the future, surely one would expect scholars and students to visit us, if such a thing were possible at all. Though they might try to disguise themselves, accidents would be bound to happen, just as they would if we went back to Imperial Rome with cameras and tape recorders concealed under our nylon togas. Time traveling could never be kept secret for very long; over and over again down the ages, chronic argonauts (to use the orginal and singularly uninspiring title of Wells's *The Time Machine*) would get into trouble and inadvertently disclose themselves.

Some science-fiction writers have tried to get around this difficulty by suggesting that Time is a spiral; though we may not be able to move along it, we can perhaps hop from coil to coil, visiting points so many millions of years apart that there is no danger of embarrassing collisions between cultures. Big-game hunters from the future may have wiped out the dinosaurs, but the age of *Homo sapiens* may lie in a blind region they cannot reach.

You will gather from this that I do not take time travel very seriously; nor, I think, does anyone else—even the writers who have devoted most effort and ingenuity to it. Yet the theme is one of the most fascinating—and sometimes the most moving—in the whole of literature, inspiring works as varied as *Jurgen* and *Berkeley Square*. It appeals to the deepest of all instincts in mankind, and for that reason it will never die.

A much less farfetched and more realistic idea than travel into the past is that we might be able to vary the rate at which we move—or appear to move—into the future. To some extent drugs already do this. For an anesthetized man, Time passes at an infinite rate. He closes his eyes for a second and opens them perhaps hours later. Stimulants can have a slight effect in the other direction, and there have been many reports of the mental acceleration, real or imagined, produced by mescaline, hashish, and other narcotics. Even if there were no undesirable side effects, such a distortion of the time sense could only be very limited. No matter how fast a man's mind operated, the sheer inertia of his body would prevent him from moving his limbs at much more than their normal speed. If you put a superfuel in the gas tank of your car, the engine will tear itself to pieces; and the body of a man is an infinitely more delicately balanced organism than an automobile engine. We may be able to slow it down to an almost unlimited extent, making possible the old dream of suspended animation and a one-way trip into the future like Rip van Winkel's. But we cannot accelerate it by means of drugs, so that a man could run a one-minute mile, or do a day's work in an hour.

Yet perhaps this could be achieved in some other way, if we draw a distinction between subjective and objective Time. The first is the Time experienced or apprehended by the human mind, which can appear to go slow or fast with varying mental states—within the limits just discussed. The second is the Time measured by such inanimate devices as clocks, oscillating crystals, or vibrating atoms; and until this century it was an act of faith among scientists that whatever *we* thought, objective Time flowed at a steady, unvarying rate. Not the least of the shocks produced by the theory of relativity was the discovery that this is simply not true.

Curiously enough, the ancient Egyptians might have found it easy to accept the relativity of Time. Their first simple sundials had faces graduated in equal arcs, so that the lengths of their "hours" necessarily varied during the day. When, some centuries later, they developed water clocks, which ran at a constant rate, they were so conditioned to the idea of variable Time that they devoted great efforts to calibrating their clocks to agree with their sundials! "In the flow of water," says Rudolf Thiel in his book *And There Was Light,* "they had a direct image of steadily flowing time. But with extraordinary skill and ingenuity they artificially produced irregularity in a regular natural phenomenon, in order to make time flow in the only manner that seemed right to them; with the inconstancy of their sundials."

The variability of Time is a natural and inevitable consequence of Einstein's discovery that Time and Space cannot be discussed separately but are aspects of a single entity, which he called Space-Time. Contrary to popular opinion, the arguments leading to this conclusion are not so abstruse and mathematical as to be beyond the layman; they are in fact so elementary as to be baffling in their very simplicity. (I wonder how often Einstein was infuriated by the phrase "Is *that* all there is to it?") The problem of explaining relativity is like that of convincing an ancient Egyptian that his water clock was really superior to his sundial, or of persuading a medieval monk that people need not fall off the other side of a spherical earth. Once preconceived ideas are cleared away, the rest is simple.

Einstein's theory holds, at any rate, that observers moving at different speeds divide up Space-Time in slightly different proportions, so that one, to put it somewhat crudely, gets a little more Time and a little less Space than the other—though the sum total is always the same. (Adding Time and Space may sound like adding apples and oranges, but we won't bother here about the mathematical trick used to do it.) Thus the rate at which Time flows in any system—inside a spaceship, for example—depends upon the speed with which that system is moving, and also upon the gravitational fields it is experiencing.

At normal speeds, and in ordinary gravitational fields, the time distortion is absolutely negligible. Even in an artificial satellite whirling round the globe at 18,000 miles an hour, a clock would lose only one tick in three billion. An astronaut making a single orbit round the Earth would have aged a millionth of a second less than his companions on the ground; the other effects of the flight would rather easily counterbalance this.

Only since 1959 has it been possible to demonstrate this incredibly tiny stretching of Time at the modest speeds of terrestrial bodies. No man-made clock could do it, but thanks to a brilliant technique evolved by the German physicist Dr. R. L. Mössbauer we can now use vibrating atoms to measure Time to an accuracy of considerably better than one part in a million million. Not, please note, one part in a million, but one part in a *million* million.

Let us pause for a moment to consider what this means, for it is another victory over Time—a metrical victory that the builders of the first sundials and water clocks could scarcely have imagined. A clock accurate to one part in a million million, which is virtually what Dr. Mössbauer has given us, would lose only one second in thirty thousand years—a single tick between the first cave painters of Lascaux and the first colonists of Mars. Such accuracy in the measurement of distance would enable us to notice if the earth's diameter increased or decreased by the thickness of a bacterium.

Although this time-stretching, or dilation, effect is so tiny at ordinary speeds, it becomes large at extraordinary ones, and very large indeed as one approaches the velocity of light. In a spaceship traveling at 87 per cent of the speed of light, or 583,234,776 miles an hour, Time would be passing at only half the rate it flows on Earth. At 99.5 per cent of the speed of light—667,032,876 miles per hour—the rate would be slowed tenfold; a month in the spaceship would be almost a year on Earth. (Relativists will, I hope, forgive me for certain oversimplifications and hidden assumptions in these statements.)

The important point to note is that there would be absolutely no way in which the space travelers could tell that anything odd was happening to them. Everything aboard the vehicle would appear to be perfectly normal—and indeed it would be. Not until they returned to Earth would they discover that far more Time had elapsed there than in the speeding ship. This is the so-called Time Paradox, which would allow, in principle at least, a man to come back to Earth centuries or millennia after he had left it, having himself aged only a few years.

The main application of this time-stretching effect is for flight to the stars, if this is ever achieved. Though such flights may last centuries, it will not seem so to the astronauts. Thus an inescapable by-product of long-range space travel is travel into the future—one-way travel, of course. An interstellar voyager could return to his own earth but never to his own age.

That such an astonishing event is possible at all would have been flatly denied fifty years ago, but now it is an accepted axiom of science. This leads us to wonder if there may not be other ways in which Time could be stretched or distorted—ways which avoid the inconvenience of traveling several light-years.

I must say at once that the prospect does not look at all hopeful. In theory, oscillation or vibration could have a similar effect on Time, but the rates involved would be so enormous that no material object could hold together under the strain. Since gravity, as well as speed, also affects the flow of Time, this line of approach looks slightly more promising. If we ever learn to control gravity, we may also learn to control Time. Once again, titanic forces would be required to produce minute time distortions. Even on the surface of a White Dwarf Star, where gravity is thousands of times more powerful than on Earth, it would require very accurate clocks to reveal that Time was running slowly.

You will have noticed that the few known means of distorting Time are not only exceedingly difficult to apply but also work in the least useful direction. Though there are occasions when we would like to slow ourselves down with

Few members of the human family have been so obsessed with Time as the Maya, whose calendar was the most accurate yet invented and who carved stone steles (like the one at right from Copán) to mark the turn of a particular series of years. This stele is thought to have been erected in A.D. 783.

DMITRI KESSEL; COURTESY Life

respect to the rest of the world, so that Time appeared to go by in a flash, the reverse process would be far more valuable. There is no one who, at some moment or other, has not felt a desperate need for more Time; often a few minutes, even a few seconds, would make the difference between life and death. Working against the clock would be no problem in a world where one could make the clock stand still, even if only for a while.

We have no idea how this might be done; neither the theory of relativity nor anything else gives us a single clue. But a *real* acceleration of Time, not the subjective and limited one produced by drugs, would be of such great value that, if it is at all possible, we will one day discover how to attain and use it. A society in which the United Nations could get through an all-day emergency session while the rest of New York had its coffee break, or in which an author could take an hour off to write an eighty-thousand-word book, is difficult to imagine and would be rather hard on the nerves. It may not be desirable and is certainly not likely; but I dare not say that it is impossible.

Traveling into the future is the one kind of time travel we all indulge in, at the steady speed of twenty-four hours every day. That we may be able to alter this rate does not, as we have seen, involve any scientific absurdities. In addition to high-speed space voyaging, suspended animation may also allow us to travel down the centuries and see what the future holds in store, beyond the normal expectation of life.

But by time travel most people mean something considerably more ambitious than that. They mean going into the future and *coming back to the present again,* preferably with a complete list of stock market quotations. This, of course, implies traveling into the past, for from the point of view of the future we are (were?) the past; and this, we have already decided, is quite impossible.

I would be willing to state that seeing into the future—clearly a less ambitious project than actually visiting it—is equally impossible, were it not for the impressive amount of evidence to the contrary. There have always, of course, been prophets and oracles who claimed the ability to foretell the future. In recent years the work of Professor J. B. Rhine at Duke University, and of Dr. Soal and his colleagues in England, has produced much more concrete proof of "precognition"—though it is all in the form of statistics, for which most people have an instinctive distrust. In this case the distrust may be justified; perhaps there is something fundamentally wrong with the mathematical analysis of the card-guessing experiments on which most claims for precognition are based. The whole subject is so complicated, and so loaded with prejudice and emotion, that I propose to tiptoe hastily away from it; if you want any more information, look up Rhine, J. B., in the card index of your local library.

Whether the future can be known, even in principle, is one of the subtlest of all philosophical questions. A century and a half ago, when Newtonian mechanics had reached its greatest triumphs in predicting the movements of the heavenly bodies, the answer was a qualified Yes. Given the initial positions and velocities of all the atoms in the universe, an all-wise mathematician could calculate everything that would happen to the end of Time. The future was predetermined down to the minutest detail, and therefore it could, in theory, be predicted.

We now know that this view is much too naïve, for it is based on a false assumption. It is *impossible* to specify the initial positions and velocities of all the atoms in the universe to the absolute degree of accuracy such a calculation would require. There is an intrinsic fuzziness, or uncertainty, about the fundamental particles, which means that we can never know exactly what they are doing at this very moment —still less a hundred years hence. Though some events— eclipses, population statistics, perhaps someday even the weather—can be predicted with considerable accuracy, the mathematical road into the future is a narrow one and eventually peters out into the quagmire of indeterminacy. If any seer or sibyl has in truth really obtained knowledge of the future, it is by some means not only unknown to present science but flatly contravening it.

Yet we know so little about Time, and have made such scanty progress in understanding and controlling it, that we cannot rule out even such outrageous possibilities as limited access to the future. Professor J. B. S. Haldane once shrewdly remarked: "The Universe is not only queerer than we imagine—it is queerer than we *can* imagine." Even the theory of relativity may only hint at the ultimate queerness of Time.

In his poem "The Future" Matthew Arnold described man as a wanderer ". . . born in a ship, / On the breast of the river of Time." Through all history that ship has been drifting rudderless and uncontrolled; now, perhaps, man is learning how to start the engines. They will never be powerful enough to overcome the current; at the best, he may delay his departure and get a better view of the lands around him and the ports he has left forever. Or he may speed up his progress and dart downstream more swiftly than the current would otherwise bear him. What he can never do is to turn back and revisit the upper reaches of the river.

And in the end, for all his efforts, it will sweep him with his hopes and dreams out into the unknown ocean:

> *As the pale waste widens around him—*
> *As the banks fade dimmer away,*
> *As the stars come out, and the night-wind*
> *Brings up the stream*
> *Murmurs and scents of the infinite sea.*

Arthur C. Clarke, a well-known writer of scientific exposition, is perhaps even better known for his works of science fiction, the latest of which is A Fall of Moondust.

BOOKS

To the Sound of Hollow Laughter

One of the trickiest problems for an author is to determine his relation to his readers. It is not always enough to start telling a story about a lot of imaginary people and expect everyone who opens the book to believe, follow, and co-operate. It is not even enough to tell the autobiographical truth and call it fiction. "Santo walked through the crowd, and was as lonely as a prisoner in a cell. The greedy faces, the hurrying bodies among whom he threaded his way, impinged upon him as little as cloud-shadows passing over a barren peak." Yes, but who cares about Santo? Are we to be impressed by him (as if his experience were something new) or to sympathize with him (although we are part of the crowd he rejects)? Why does the author trouble to walk into our home and tell us a long yarn about a total stranger? and why do we listen? why do we believe?

Many of us listen because we enjoy vicarious experience. On an evening walk, we pass a house on the roadside. If it has a window lit and uncurtained, we cannot resist looking in. To glance into another person's life makes our own private world a little richer. Yes, but suppose at the second glance we realize that the figures inside are not behaving naturally. Expecting to be spied upon, and hearing our footsteps, they have put on a little show. The man is standing on his head in a Yoga posture; the woman is painting a picture in mid-air with a brush but no canvas; they wear a bogus air of seriousness on their faces, and their lips are twitching. At once we walk away, indignant with them and ashamed of ourselves for being taken in.

Most fiction pretends to be "real": the characters have a recognizable, comprehensible life that we can share. While we read, we believe. The author himself, while he writes, also frequently believes. But there are certain stories that are contrived, and are meant to seem contrived. Volubly though their characters talk, dramatically though they gesticulate, they are acting parts in which the actors do not believe. And their producer, the novelist, What does he think of them? and of us?

Vladimir Vladimirovich Nabokov is such a novelist. His latest book, *Pale Fire* (Putnam, 1962), is not his best, but it is one of his strangest; and it is strange in this special way. No one else could have written it, and scarcely any-one else would even have thought of writing it.

It is, or rather it pretends to be, a poem written by an American poet, published with a commentary by an expatriate European scholar; and the gimmick is that the commentary is all rubbish. Not only has it nothing to do with the matter and style of the poem, but it grows into an elaborate imaginative structure that is obviously absurd.

A few details will make things clearer. Nabokov gives us the story of two people: one sane and dead, the other insane and alive. The dead person is the old poet John Francis Shade. He was shot by an escaped lunatic; but he had finished, or almost finished, a handsome poem called *Pale Fire*—an autobiographical meditation in "heroic" couplets, in style and concept not unlike John Betjeman's recent *Summoned by Bells*. The survivor, Dr. Charles Kinbote, comes from the European country of Zembla, which in some ways resembles Sweden. He is a philologist, lecturing for a year at Wordsmith College in New England; tall, bearded, vegetarian, inquisitive, endlessly garrulous, paranoiac, and homosexual. Having rented the house next door to Shade, he endeavors to move into Shade's life, taking him for walks, begging for invitations into his home, and when rebuffed, spying on him with maniacal persistence. When the old man tells him he is starting a poem, Kinbote actually suggests a subject to him—an absurd melodrama about an assassin's pursuit of an exiled Zemblan monarch. After Shade's murder, Kinbote gets the poet's distracted widow to assign him editorial rights, and flees with the manuscript to a lonely place in the Rocky Mountains. There, without companions or advisers, he composes this gigantic commentary, which occupies most of the book. Almost wholly irrelevant, the commentary shows that Kinbote has no real interest in Shade's poetry or understanding of it. The very title, *Pale Fire,* comes from Shakespeare (*Timon of Athens,* 4.3.444); but Kinbote cannot identify it because, out there in Utana near the Idoming border, he has no library. He has a copy of *Timon of Athens,* translated into Zemblan by Zembla's national poet, but cannot trace the quotation there.

Instead of actually explicating the text of the poem, Kinbote uses it as a framework from which to draw three stories: the story of his own lonely unhappiness at Wordsmith College (relieved only by his admiration for Shade), the outline of Shade's life while he is working on *Pale Fire* (with flashbacks), and the melodramatic escape-and-pursuit tale of King Charles of Zembla and the murderer Gradus. The stories interlock, although for some time it is difficult to see what the adventures of the king of Zembla have to do with the peaceful life of New England. But Kinbote keeps hinting at it, until he lets it out. He believes he himself is King Charles; he believes the escaped lunatic was a revolutionary agent who was sent to kill him and blew a hole in the poet by mistake.

This novel is clearly a little masterpiece of ingenuity. Shade's poem itself is charming. The gradual self-exposure of Kinbote's insane mind is skillful. There is even some comic suspense and excitement, as the assassin approaches (suffering from diarrhea), and as the maniac escapes to the mountains clutching the precious poem. The prose style is that lavish *pâté-terrine de foie gras* which is Nabokov's speciality, interlined with truffles, cloves, parsley, salt pork, mace, black pepper, and one or two bay leaves. Both his poet and his philologer love words: they play a fine game called "word golf"; and the pages of the book glitter with such verbal gems as "comedo," "fatidic," "iridule," "lemniscate," "preterist," "stang," and "stillicide." One might say that such an author does not work by the customary parameters, and if his epigrams were less glochidiate one might suspect him of deliberate steganography. The phrase "an undeodorized Frenchwoman" would have pleased Joris-Karl Huysmans, who could tell a blonde fellow countrywoman from a brunette with his eyes closed; and a skyscraper at night is well described as a "luminous waffle."

The point of the book? It has several, as the best fictional satire should have; and it is best understood by comparisons with Nabokov's previous novels. Like *Lolita,* it is a study in obsessional insanity, particularly in its power to systematize the indeterminate, to make a gruesome work of art out of random and even mean elements. (The arch and cloying sentimentality of the male homosexual, waved like a camellia-scented handkerchief in so many recent novels and poems, is elegantly spoofed.) Like Nabokov's *Pnin,* it is a satire on the European intellectual in America, who feels himself an aristocrat rudely jostled by the lower middle class. Like his *The Real Life of Sebastian Knight,* it is the reconstruction of a dead author's life through a study of his work and milieu.

But it is also a farcical caricature of scholarship. How many commentaries there are that explain the obvious and reproach the author for minor errors of taste! And now we have a commentary that is almost completely irrelevant and attempts to redesign the entire poem it sets out to discuss. Then again, it is a satiric study of the literary parasite, who is tolerated because of his persistence (or in spite of it), who helps a great man to feel he is great, and who lightens the loneliness of genius. Boswell and Johnson, Eckermann and Goethe, there have been many such couples; but who knows how often, and how seriously, the parasite has distorted the true character of his host?

Vladimir Nabokov is a tease. How far is he teasing his readers? Consider, first, his elaborate vocabulary. Such words as "gloam" and "torquated" are, although recherché, genuine. But what are we to say when his characters make errors in English? There is no such word as Nabokov's "widowery": its sound alone condemns it. No sensitive writer could say that he *entitled* a book *with* a phrase. A New England poet would not write "we luncheoned," which is plausible only for the secretary of a society-ladies' club. Of course, no one's ear is impeccable: even Tennyson said he did not know the metrical value of the word "scissors." But are these and other locutions genuine mistakes that have slipped past Mr. Nabokov's corrective pen? Or are they blunders that he thinks characteristic of his polyglot alien and his polymath poet? Or, conceivably, are they errors he inserts because he despises us, his readers? Will he chuckle as he reads reviews praising his remarkable grasp of English and his delicate stylistic sense, and recalls that he laid several booby traps?

The sensitive reader dislikes being teased, unless it is done with such tact and good humor as in *Tristram Shandy.* He is apt to resent an author who keeps saying, "Look, how clever I am! Here's a puzzle. I thought you'd miss it. I bet you can't solve it. There's another one inside. And inside that. . . ." Few except paid specialists or unpaid masochists read Joyce's *Finnegans Wake* and Lycophron's *Alexandra.* What are we to feel when we read *Pale Fire* and are asked to believe that the commentator's name, Kinbote, means "King-Killer" in Zemblan and that he signs his name with the design of a black chess-king? and when we remember that one of

Nabokov's earlier novels had a hero whose chosen symbol was a chess knight and whose mistress was called Bishop? Yet, apart from these minor subtleties, is the novel itself credible? The poem is, certainly. But do we believe that a poet who was rather like Robert Frost would really tolerate the pawings and mouthings of a crank? or that his widow would allow his beloved last poem to be whipped away from her and then published in such a manner as almost to ruin it? Are we even expected to give credit to all this? Or is Nabokov playing an elaborate joke on us, a joke only he can fully enjoy?

Recently I reread Nabokov's early fantasy, *Invitation to a Beheading*. It begins with a man's condemnation to death and ends with his execution by guillotine, and is full of grotesque impossibilities that are both comical and gloomy. In the condemned cell the prisoner takes off all his clothes, and then takes off his head and his torso and his limbs, and dissolves. But when the jailer unbolts the door, he instantly takes his full physical shape again. This is incredible, not meant to be believed, but true and meaningful. So a prisoner will think himself out of his cage and out of his captive body until he is recalled to a reality no less absurd. *Lolita*, too, was incredible, and its ending was ludicrous; yet its lustful plot and its jocular style produced a hideously painful effect, like the laughter of hysteria. Nowadays we think it cruel to laugh at deformity and lunacy. Nabokov tries to make us do so. Meanwhile he watches us with a pale stare in which there is more contempt than pity.   GILBERT HIGHET

THEATRE

A Coming Talent Casts its Shadow Before

Astute medicine men win reputations for chumminess with the gods by authorizing rain dances when the direction of the wind, the season of the year and, if possible, a phone call to the weather bureau suggest that the ceremony will be effective. I shall try to gain a similar reputation for influence within the high councils of the American theatre by calling for an early production of the plays of John Arden, only one of which has been staged professionally in the United States, in San Francisco. In this case, there is no bureau to check, but my plea should have a good chance: our producers are not so burdened with golden opportunities that they can overlook for long a talent as strong and varied as this.

John Arden—aged thirty-two—is a young English dramatist whose plays, like those of so many of his contemporaries, have been staged in London at the Royal Court Theatre. No one writing about the contemporary theatre can avoid an appearance of Anglophilia. Americans are writing good plays, but talent does not flourish here in a concentration comparable to what prevails in England. John Osborne, Arnold Wesker, Harold Pinter, Shelagh Delaney, Brendan Behan, N. F. Simpson, John Mortimer, Willis Hall, John Arden —the roster proves the point, and this does not exhaust the names. I don't know why this fecundity has come about, but the Royal Court and Joan Littlewood's Theatre Workshop (at present suspended) may have something to do with it. If you let it be known that you respect new ideas and fresh approaches, that you are willing to take a flyer on a long shot, you are at least more likely to get them. Aside from that, the stage has always been the Englishman's castle, and there is nothing inherently surprising about its current vitality there.

The Arden plays thus far are *Live Like Pigs, Serjeant Musgrave's Dance,* and *The Happy Haven* (there is a still earlier work, *The Waters of Babylon*, but it was given only in a single special performance). The first thing that almost everyone says of these plays is that they could very plausibly be the writings of three different men. *Live Like Pigs* is an earthy, raucous comic strip in seventeen scenes; *Serjeant Musgrave's Dance* is a somber historical drama in three acts; *The Happy Haven* is a two-act fantasy with overtones of surrealist horror. This diversity of attack is quite deliberate. Arden has a gift for looking at his career objectively. For example, he has known since the age of sixteen that he wanted to write, but he spent his years at Cambridge and Edinburgh training himself as an architect and thereafter worked two years in an architect's office. He says he didn't "know any *way* of becoming a writer," and he did know the way to become an architect. If the writing succeeded, he could always get out of the building profession; if it did not, he had a calling that would support his family. Arden is a poet and a dreamer, but a prudent one: there is something peculiarly Anglo-Saxon about that.

Part of his prudence, evidently, is to serve his theatre apprenticeship by writing as many kinds of plays as he can devise. In this he is quite unlike many of his colleagues—especially Wesker and Pinter, whose signatures are very strong on their plays—and he is paying a price for the experience gained. Arden's critical reputation far exceeds his commercial success: the major applause for each of his plays has come after the production closed, with only a moderate run. If he had picked a last and stuck to it, he would probably have profited from the momentum of acclaim; that is how his fellows have built such large followings so quickly. But Arden has come on stage each time with a "first" play.

Despite this calculated eclecticism, there is consistency in Arden's work if you look for it. There is, first, the matter of his language. His characters speak a stylized vernacular; that is, the dialogue is much sharper and more allusive than real speech, but it sounds "fitting" in the mouths for which it is designed. For example, this speech from Act I of *Serjeant Musgrave's Dance:*

MUSGRAVE. There was talk about danger. Well, I never heard of no danger yet that wasn't comparative. Compare it against your purposes. And compare it against my strategy. Remember: the roads are closed, the water's frozen, the telegraph wires are weighted down with snow, they haven't *built* the railway. We came here safe, and here we are, safe here. The winter's giving us one day, two days, three days even— that's clear safe for us to hold our time, take count of the corruption, then stand before this people with our white shining word, and let it dance! It's a hot coal, this town, despite that it's freezing—choose your minute and blow: and whoosh, she's flamed your roof off!

At the same time, however, Arden uses song (in the manner of Brecht, though I should think by way of Brendan Behan), and he uses verse. When the emotional content of a scene exceeds a certain intensity, or when he wants a detail pulled forward, as though sharpened by a lens, Arden turns to poetry. It is an effective device, for it is a frank avowal that the theatre is art and not life. By going directly into poetry, Arden spares himself the incongruous "fine sentiments" that result when an author tries to speak for himself through the normal accents of his characters, and that so often ring like lead on the realistic stage. Most of the scenes in *Live Like Pigs* are introduced by songs or spoken quatrains, which state the theme for what is to follow. The song at the opening of Scene V is:

They build a wall to keep you in,
It serves to keep them out.
So when they set their feet on the wall
Beware what you're about.

In subject matter, too, there is congruity beneath Arden's variety. Two of his plays (and possibly the others as well) were touched off by actual events. He wrote *Live Like Pigs* after reading of a riot that occurred in a northern industrial housing development; and *Serjeant Musgrave's Dance,* though set in the 1860's, was inspired by a massacre that took place one night during the terror on Cyprus. An Arden plot is characteristically a specific moral or social dilemma, and what marks it as his work is that he respects dilemmas too much to solve them by some theatrical presto chango. It takes unusual maturity, particularly in this age of social manipulation and psychological rehabilitation, to recognize that cutting the Gordian knot is always a cheap dramatic trick. It also requires great technical skill to bring a play to a satisfactory end without pretending to dispose of the problem it raises. Arden's plays do not offer the last word—which may be another reason why they have not set box-office records. Audiences must accustom themselves to the fact that he promises no revelations and guarantees no cures; he is a dramatist of the intractability of life.

If I were sponsoring Arden in this country (this offering of unsolicited advice is great fun), I should open with *Serjeant Musgrave's Dance* (recently published by Grove Press). It is not the easiest of his plays, but it is the most substantial and the one that can exert the greatest impact on an audience. The time is the Crimean War. Serjeant Musgrave and three troopers under his spell have deserted after participating in a peculiarly pointless massacre, and have returned to England—posing as a recruiting unit—to let their countrymen know the reality of war. They make for a particular mining town because, as we eventually discover, they carry with them the skeleton of one of their mates who was a youth from that town. It is their plan to display this relic as a symbol of the road to glory—and Musgrave has in mind other devices of direct and terrible logic (scarcely guessed at by his henchmen) to drive the lesson home. What gives the play its power and its present relevance is that Musgrave is a *religious* man. He is akin to those Cromwellian troopers who carried Bibles in their knapsacks and worshiped a God of Wrath. Musgrave wants peace, but he wants to impose it by the sword; and of course he is a man accursed, one who carries violence like a contagion.

Serjeant Musgrave's Dance is built as a sculptor builds in clay: handful by handful the material is laid up, and gradually the composition takes on mass and shape and the tension that gives it life. Plot, character, background—all parts of the play grow simultaneously, and it is perhaps at its greatest power as it comes to its conclusion. It is a play that must be directed plastically, in space rather than in time, and with each moment exploited for its own quality as much as for its contribution to the total object. Arden provides good clay—he is lavish with humor, violence, suspense, vivid personalities, high jinks, and deviltry. But the play carries, thus, a good deal of baggage and, since it is not hauled forward by an urgent narrative, it could bog down. If its details are relished, however, and if it is staged with a material richness (the costumes

The characters in John Arden's plays carry harsh conflicts within themselves. Serjeant Musgrave (left) is by training a soldier and by instinct a man of God; the old people in The Happy Haven—*played by young actors who wear masks (above)—want to live long but are afraid when offered a serum enabling them to do so; and the impoverished family in* Live Like Pigs *(right) is put into a comfortable house—which they hate.*

should be vivid, the furniture solid) and a vigor of motion to match its stature, it will build tremendous momentum. It needs the money and the professional polish of a Broadway production.

*Live Like Pigs,** on the contrary, would go like a breeze off Broadway. It demands quick wits and a rough agility, but not much in the way of appointments. If *Serjeant Musgrave* is heroic clay, *Live Like Pigs* is ironic cartooning. Its central character is the Sawney family, described thus by Arden in an introduction: "The Sawneys are an anachronism. They are the direct descendants of the 'sturdy beggars' of the sixteenth century, and the apparent chaos of their lives becomes an ordered pattern when seen in terms of a wild, empty countryside and a nomadic existence. Put out of their fields by enclosing landlords, they found such an existence possible for four hundred years. Today, quite simply, there are too many buildings in England, and there is just no room for nomads. The family in this play fails to understand this, and becomes educated in what is known as the 'hard way,' but which might also be called the 'inefficient way.'"

As the play opens, Sailor Sawney, his wife Big Rachel, her son Col, his daughter Rosie, and Rosie's daughter Sally

* Published by Penguin Books in the collection *New English Dramatists 3* but not distributed in the United States.

have been evicted from the derelict tramcar in which they resided and have been installed by the authorities in a housing project. They are shortly joined by Blackmouth, a half-mad half-Gypsy who is the father of Rosie's children; by The Old Croaker, a crone of senile craftiness; and by Daffodil, her deformed but avid daughter. Next door live the Jacksons—husband, wife, and salesclerk-daughter—a family self-intoxicated with lower-middle-class respectability. One gathers that the neighborhood is rife with such as they.

The Sawney tribe of thieves, whores, drunks, and roisterers did not choose to be housed in genteel digs; they do not propose to moderate their old manners to their new surroundings. And the smallest, the oldest, the feeblest, or the dottiest of the Sawneys is more than a match for the best the Jacksons can put forward. Four hundred years of quick jabs and billingsgate are not wiped out by a fortnight in a "model" home. But the Jacksons have a terrible weapon unknown to the Sawneys: they can organize, and having done so, they can roll over nonconformity and crush it flat. And they do.

One could milk a good deal of pathos out of this situation—natural exuberance at bay, the end of romance, the

juggernaut of propriety grinding out the last sparks of individuality. It is clear, however, that Arden intends no such sniveling. The Sawneys are scarcely to be equated with the noble savage; they are sadly, if also comically, neurotic victims of injustice that dates back four centuries. Their roaring and lusting look attractive only in juxtaposition to the mealy pretensions of Jacksonian aridity, and in fact they are half-starved, wholly ignorant, a plague to themselves and to anyone they encounter. Their life of dreams is pulled down by people no better than they—only more modern. It may not be progress (though a little crossbreeding between the Sawneys and the Jacksons *could* be enlivening), but it is certainly inevitable.

Live Like Pigs is a lark, bitter but uproarious, to commemorate the passing of a breed that never did more than make a virtue of adversity. It should be staged as a burlesque show—hard, fast, rancid, knowing, essentially innocent, and with complete sympathy and no pity at all.

About *The Happy Haven* (unpublished as yet) I am less certain—perhaps because it is a kind of play I do not find congenial, but also because it is a little slippery as to content. It is a dark fantasy, a cautionary fairy tale for adults. Happy Haven is an old folks' home, run by a doctor (half mad-scientist, half supersalesman) who has discovered an elixir of youth. His inmates are to be his guinea pigs. Now you might suppose that these octogenarian ladies and gents would snap at a chance to sample the doctor's brew, but it turns out that they want no part of it; and when a test draught works with spectacular success on an invisible dog that has been cavorting around the stage all evening, they turn on the calculating humanitarian and dose him with his own medicine.

The style of the play is modified Grand Guignol, with the decent façades of the aged pensioners slipping from time to time to allow a glimpse of monstrosities within. It is quite brilliant in tone (in a way, it is virtuoso dialogue, but not always in a good way); the point, however, seems to me to blur. One of the old crocks, himself excluded from rejuvenation because of a physical impediment, convinces the others that their lives have been far too miserable

to be lived over again. That does not persuade me, on the other hand, for Arden has given his aged crew such a determined grasp on life that they would obviously leap at the prospect of running the course again.

What could have enraged them, and urged them to turn the tables on the doctor, is the discovery that they are not being cared for but used. No man grows so old, so feeble, so useless, that he will consent to being regarded as an object—it is a sin against the soul and not to be tolerated even in exchange for life everlasting. But that is only what one supposes from meeting Arden's company—there is no support for this thesis in the text.

The Happy Haven was played in London in masks. Arden felt that it would be cruel to ask actors of an age comparable to those of the characters to play such parts (but aren't elderly actors accustomed to taking parts beset by age?); at any event, the action is so athletic that genuinely old people could not possibly sustain it, and so he puts

masks on youngsters. He would have profited from seeing Sudie Bond play Grandma in Albee's *The American Dream*. That play is also a fantasy: it puts no value on realistic illusion, and Miss Bond did not pretend to be Dame Sybil Thorndike. She played a caricature, as did everyone in *The American Dream*, and as everyone must in *The Happy Haven*. But if you add the exaggeration of masks to what are already caricatures, you must double the stimulus in a confusing way. Some such confusion evidently did bedevil the London production.

I keep my fingers crossed, then, about *The Happy Haven*—at least, I'd be in no great rush to import it. But *Serjeant Musgrave's Dance* would lend stature and *Live Like Pigs* would lend effervescence to any season in which they appeared. They are not easy to stage, but the theatre is not an exercise in rolling off a log. They would repay the labor and brains that were invested in them—and of how many new plays can that be said?   ROBERT HATCH

CHANNELS

Television Culture in Round Numbers

This column, or at least a good deal of it, is going to be devoted to numbers. I wish to warn the faithful that there will be considerable division and subtraction and other like indignities. This is a most discouraging prospect, but I shall round off the larger sums and generally seek to be merciful. Numbers then.

The first number I wish to present is 2,000,000. I did not choose it; I do not really know who did, but it turns out to be the number of dollars that will be

available to Channel 13, New York, for its first year of operation as an educational television station.

With part of that money Channel 13 will be called upon to provide classroom television for the thirsting tots of New York, New Jersey, and Connecticut. This has been budgeted at $750,000, leaving the handsome sum of $1,250,000 for all other purposes. Among those other purposes is the provision of eight and a half hours of cultural broadcast-

ing six days a week between the hours of 3:30 P.M. and midnight. Calculating rapidly on my fingers, I find that comes to about $500 per hour of culture.

We have now arrived at a remarkable number, conducive to deep thought. For example, $500 is very nearly the total production cost of five seconds of a *Bob Hope Show*. But of course that is quite unreasonable: *The Bob Hope Show* puts out a pretty penny for what is carelessly called "talent" and goes out over a nationwide network; it has a far larger audience even in Greater New York, which should know better, than Channel 13 will ever have. I shouldn't have brought it up in the first place.

Let us consider *CBS Reports* instead. This is a carefully prepared, carefully produced, beautifully presented documentary show, the tone and style of which are exactly what a good educational station should want to capture. On an educational channel, of course, subject and treatment might differ widely from that of *CBS Reports*, but the level of excellence should be comparable. It must be comparable. Well, Channel 13's $500 might buy as much as fifteen seconds of *CBS Reports*.

Or we can approach the matter in another fashion. Let us assume that Channel 13, after deep thought, decides to bring its viewers a videotape of Leonard Bernstein rehearsing the New York Philharmonic for one of its performances—a two-hour program in which some of the problems and pleasures of whipping a concert into shape might be presented to an audience of music lovers and the plain curious. While we are being so free with our assumptions, let us assume also that neither Bernstein nor his orchestra would ask so much as a thin dime for its part in the act. The best estimate I can get from those who are accustomed to perform this sort of task is that salaries, wages, and materials adequate to do the job really properly would come to something like $6,000. (I might add hastily that I see absolutely no reason why Bernstein and the orchestra should be asked to work free, but when I assume, I go the limit.) Unless my fingers deceive me, the $1,000 that Channel 13 has available for two hours would actually buy them twenty minutes, provided that everyone at Channel 13 worked for nothing too.

Maybe all this is too esoteric. I can put it in quite ordinary terms. The production of a television program is—or should be—a creative act. It requires thought and preparation, false starts, and discarded inspirations. Because it is so intensely collaborative, it demands the participation over a significant period of time of a great number of able and talented persons. Offhand I can think of nothing with which it can be equated, but it is clearly a major effort. Very well—$500 will buy approximately five days of a first-rate talent's time, if he doesn't mind working cheap for a good cause. This leaves nothing for preparing the show, running the station, paying the help, and providing sugar for the coffee breaks.

It all adds up to a promise that Channel 13 will dispense the same bedraggled trash and pompous boredom that are the staple fare of educational television wherever it exists in the United States. We may look forward to thirty minutes of "The Art of Paper Folding," followed by thirty minutes of a bored professor showing slides of paramecia, followed by an hour-long panel show to which even the panelists pay no marked attention.

Because Channel 13 has already collected more than its share of first-rate persons with a real devotion to what they are about, it won't all be like that. I am sure there will be programs that set new standards for educational television, and nothing in the world needs new standards more than educational television does. But the price of every respectable program will be half a dozen hours of film from the National Educational Television library, most of which was miserable stuff even before it got scratched and dirty.

You only get the full horror of this when you measure it against the opportunity. The world doesn't possess a gold mine for educational television comparable to New York, with its theatres and its museums; its music and its dance; its concentration of creative talent in all the arts, the humanities, and the sciences; its constant stream of distinguished men and women. This exciting real world is now almost totally ignored by commercial television, which finds it gets more mileage out of the never-never land of the Hollywood Sound Stage and Central Casting.

Film and videotape are relatively cheap, once production costs are paid.

A New York station that was really a flag station could revivify noncommercial television from coast to coast, creating a fourth network that might never cut deeply into the audiences of the three commercial networks but might very well command its two or three or ten million faithful viewers.

But it will never happen until educational television faces up to the fact that, culture or mayhem, television is show business. The cultural program requires the same solicitous preparation and the same dedicated production as *The Untouchables*. It never has to be as expensive as a spectacular, because brains don't command the same financial rewards as busts, but where programs are comparable—in narrative flow, in the techniques of getting a picture on the air, in attention to detail— the cultural program has to match up to the commercial program. One touch of shoddy taints the whole product, and even the man who desperately wants to watch the "good" program will find himself honestly incapable of doing so.

Educational television has to pay for talented staff, because even a devoted man has a wife and children, and perhaps a hankering for wall-to-wall carpets; and if he has talent, he will inevitably be seduced by commercial television.

I can sum it up. A bad show is a bad show, whether it is called *The United Nations—Moments of Decision* or *Father Knows Best*. And the numbers presented above commit Channel 13 to bad shows, just as surely as the Weather Girl follows the News.

Which brings me back to the subject of numbers, and I happen to have one more number to submit: during 1960 (which is the latest year for which figures are available) Procter & Gamble spent $100 million in commercial television. But I see that I have fallen victim to my habit of rounding off numbers; to be more nearly accurate, Procter & Gamble spent $102 million. I'm sorry—when you are selling soap, an extra $2 million scarcely seems worth mentioning.   STEPHEN WHITE

AMATEURS ALL

A hitherto unpublished speech, before the Moscow Party Congress, by Chairman N. S. Khrushchev

The Soviet Union plans to issue a challenge for the America's Cup, which United States Yachtsmen have successfully defended since 1851. Aleksei Promislov, the President of the Soviet Yachting Federation, said today that a formal challenge would be made in 1964. Australia will compete against the United States for the cup this year. Britain will seek it in 1963. . . . The British have spent close to $20,000,000 trying to regain the inexpensive cup, which was known as the 100-Guinea Cup when the Schooner America won it in a race around the Isle of Wight in 1851. In the last challenge in 1958, the British yacht Sceptre was soundly trounced by the United States defender, Columbia, in four straight races. . . . As long as the United States holds the America's Cup, challenges for it must be directed to the New York Yacht Club. . . . Challenges may not emanate directly from a nation as such but must be filed by a recognized yacht club. . . .

—From an Associated Press despatch

Comrades! Ahoy!

(Laughter in the hall)

Comrades! You are asking yourselves, what has happened to Nikita Sergeievitch? Why does he wear this silly cap? What is this bourgeois coat with the imperialist brass buttons? What are these creamy counterrevolutionary pants? Why these White-Terror shoes? Who is this vulgar boatman, this nautical enemy of the people?

(Further animation in the hall)

Let me remind you, comrades, of an old folk-saying. He who is noticed laughing last, laughs in the Lubyanka.

(Silence in the hall)

Thank you.

Fellow workers and peasants, do not be deceived. These are not the garments of decadent capitalism but the uniform of the Commodore of the great Sovietskii Gosudarstvennyi Vostanovitelnyi Yacht Klub, SovGosVos, the Soviet people's recreational yacht club, an honored position to which, surprised as I am, I will be elected tomorrow. I, the son of a humble coal miner!

You ask, comrades, what have we to do with yacht clubs? I answer you that in everything Socialism must be first: in power, in science, in sport, even for the prize most highly valued by the oppressed capitalist seafarers, the famous America's Cup. We will take this cup, we will fill this cup with vodka, we will make it the *Russia*'s Cup.

(Enthusiasm in the hall)

No student of propaganda should fail to notice how powerful a figure is the Great Sailor, in any age, from Columbus to our great Gagarin, the Sailor of Space! How was the well-known Roosevelt photographed? With a sailor's cape. What is

By OLIVER JENSEN

the sport of the noted American politician Kennedy and the Englishman Edinburgh? Sailing little boats. The English kings frequently dress as admirals: it is an image drawn from ancient history, the ship of state, its leader at the helm. A shrewd propaganda by the exploiters. And there is an old saying in the Donbas, that when you see a good idea, steal it.

But there is a difficulty, for the imperialist powers who race for this cup also make the rules. The governments do not race, or even challenge. This last rite is performed by "yacht clubs," and the racers are "amateurs," a word very hard to translate into our Soviet language. The pretense is that it is all private and unprofessional. And that is why, to challenge for this prize, we too must have an official All-Union amateur yacht club.

Shortsighted comrades will object that the yachting class was foreign to the spirit of Marxism-Leninism, and was liquidated. This is, however, a negativistic view, born of incorrect thinking. Let us study the words of Marx, who tells us that the capitalist does no labor, and grows rich on the unpaid labor of other men. But I invite your attention to the reverse situation, which exists among the yachtniks: the owners of the yachts work very hard, and pay large sums to many other men, for no visible economic reward. The sport is wet, and cold. Who do the yachtniks oppress? Themselves! Clearly, therefore, the yachtnik is not a capitalist. Dialectical science thus proves that opponents of the yachting five-year plan are guilty of faulty principles. To paraphrase Lenin, therefore, the Soviet Union equals Socialism plus sailboats.

Now, as a result, our great shipyards are building yachts to compete in this race. Factory soviets, Komsomols, and Kolkhozes are setting up SovGosVos clubs. Norms are being exceeded; indeed, norms are always exceeded. For what else are they? Cadres of helm-workers, halyard-workers, and line-handlers, both Starboardites and Portoviki, are being trained. Our Great Soviet Academy is studying the signals and decoding the code flags of the Western sailors, and a special commission is preparing translations of such difficult terms as "amateur." It is part of the linguistic sabotage of the imperialists to devise words like "fo'c'sle," "luffing," and "guinea" to confuse honest workers; it is probable that the last is some kind of racial epithet directed at their Negroes, who are frequently lynched, as is well known, by a rope we believe is known as a "Topsy," or "Topping Lift." Further reports are expected, but it is already known that they have *Race Committees*. Is this not suspicious? We are also investigating a sinister practice known as *splicing the main brace;* it relates to something brought up from the galley, and may involve the presence of galley slaves and other colonialist activities. In any case Radio Moscow is already describing these criminal acts over our African and Asian broadcasts.

Comrades! You cannot make a revolution without breaking precedents. We are not hunting kulaks any more. We are not rowing little boats. Our brave yachtsmen who go to sail with the foreigners must learn their ways, although of course they will leave their relatives behind here in Russia in case they learn them too well. First of all, they must learn to say they are *not* yachting workers, but something else. For instance Popov is a coal miner, Ivanov a sewer *aktiv*, Nikolaev a porter—but all are amateur yachtniks. Do not smile, comrades, for the Americans will believe anything. And there is the matter of the engines in the boats, which must not be used during the races, impractical as this may sound. At least, the officials must not discover that they are being used, which they will detect if some wrecker is foolish enough to move along briskly when the sea is flat calm. I am told that in yachting circles engines are sealed before races and inspected afterward to see whether the seals have been broken. Our position on inspection, however, is well known. Despite the imperialist propaganda, a disguise for espionage, we are in favor of inspection; I refer to self-inspection. To show how fair we are, we will have a political commissar on the Soviet boat, and he will perform the inspection. If there are objections, we will propose a round of toasts. If they continue arguing, we will continue toasting. Co-exist at the bar until they drop!

Remember also, the Americans and the Englishmen are peculiar people, with strange customs. They chase foxes, for example, on horses, with packs of dogs and no guns. They do not even bother to remove the fences or walls. A sensible man would say it is easier to shoot or trap the foxes, but that would not be what they call "sporting." In England it is said men play at games for the sport alone, and pretend they do not care at all if they lose. In their sports these people have rules about "fouls," like crowding other boats in sailing or a thing like "buzzing" by our brave fighter pilots in the Berlin corridors; but they do not like to claim them very often. Doubtless it is another sign of their decadence.

Heroes of Soviet Yachting, sail to victory! Grasp the helm! Pull the line! Seize the fair wind! Claim the foul! Unless out of sight of other vessels, pick up survivors! Interrogate them! Bring the cup back to the Soviet Fatherland! And do not forget the old saying, "There is no second." Especially in Moscow.

(*Pandemonium*)

Alfred Kazin:

The Critic as Creator

"At its best, true literary criticism may actually suggest new subjects, can enliven the imagination. . . . Its greatest single attribute is its force, its passionate declaration of the true nature of man and what his proper destiny may be."

—Kazin in "Contemporaries" (1962)

The view of the critic as a creative person—a man constructing his own vision of his times—has become more acceptable in Europe than in America, where so many of the critics seem content merely to analyze the work of art before them and pass a carefully limited judgment, and where even the most dubious poets and story writers are thought to be engaged in something called "creative writing"—though scarcely ever a critic. However, since he made his reputation in the early forties—with his long study of American prose called On Native Grounds—*Alfred Kazin has been one of the handful of American critics who insist that the arts can be revealed to us only if we see them "against the background of man's striving."*

It seems predictable, then, that a reader turning through the pages of Kazin's new book Contemporaries *will find himself leaping across a range of subjects that most literary scholars today would find altogether risky, if not outrageous, in their variety. Kazin's previous books have been almost equally diverse:* A Walker in the City *(1951) was a long evocation of his youth in the Brooklyn ghetto;* The Inmost Leaf *(1955) began with a lengthy study of Blake and finished with one of Faulkner.*

Kazin works at his craft. He lives comfortably on Manhattan's upper West Side with his wife and daughter, but early each morning he goes downtown to a small studio on Fourteenth Street and seldom leaves before 5 or 6 P.M. The little flat once belonged to an artist and has been kept quite sparsely furnished: a day bed, neatly piled with magazines like Commentary *and the* New Statesman; *a desk and bookshelves; and on the walls some oils left by the departed painter.*

This rather cozy studio nonetheless represents a kind of triumph. At a time when some American critics work over their specialities in universities, Kazin has been able to establish himself as a "man of letters" in the European sense of an independent commentator on the state of society, on the cultural past, on new work in the arts. Editors of maga-

An interview by ROBERT B. SILVERS

zines and publishing houses often ask him to write, and colleges to lecture. And as this interview would seem to show, Kazin's very demanding but independent situation is appropriate to his work itself. For in his view there are no safe limits to the things the good critic must seek to know, nor to the responsibilities he must embrace.

INTERVIEWER: Just twenty years ago you established yourself as a critic at the age of twenty-seven with your book *On Native Grounds*. Looking back, I wonder how you came to write criticism at all.

KAZIN: In fact, I was twenty-two when I started that book—around 1937. I was taking an M.A. in history at Columbia, and at the same time I had been doing some book reviews for the New York *Times* and the *Herald Tribune*. One day Carl van Doren, who worked as an adviser to Reynal & Hitchcock, suggested that instead of looking for a teaching job I should do a book on modern American writing. He said I needed a book, not a job, and he was quite right. His suggestion changed my life.

INTERVIEWER: It hadn't entered your mind until then?

KAZIN: No, I had no plan at all to write such a book, and when Van Doren asked me to try, it was like the sudden discovery of a vocation. Somewhat to my surprise I saw immediately the shape of a book on the rise of modern literature in America—it was as if the nature of the book had been buried in me, waiting to be awakened.

INTERVIEWER: How do you explain this quick transition from history to literary criticism?

KAZIN: It really wasn't a transition at all. In a sense I had been unconsciously preparing to do such a book since I was a boy. I think the most important single influence on me was the fact that I was a Jew who grew up in the immigrant world of Brooklyn, the son of very poor Russian Jewish working people—my mother worked as a dressmaker, my father as a house painter. Now that was an extraordinary world to grow up in:

not only did it have deep respect for the traditions of European learning, but it was filled with intellectual passions—above all the passion for a just society. And it was a world filled with the immigrants' sense of America—of American history as a process by which the good society might at last be realized. So as I went from City College to Columbia, in the middle of the Depression, it was inconceivable to me that I could be simply an academic specialist in history. I was swept up in all sorts of socialist and radical ideas, and I believed that modern art and modern history had come to be very much related.

INTERVIEWER: How, specifically, did you see them as related?

KAZIN: I felt that the great American writers of the 1920's whom I'd been admiring since high school—people like Hemingway and Dreiser and Sherwood Anderson and Edmund Wilson—represented part of a continuing, hopeful, forward movement in American life, a movement that had its roots in the independent visions of nineteenth-century American prophets like Emerson and Lincoln and Whitman. And it wasn't only the writers of the twenties who had this impact on me, but also painters like John Marin and the photographer Alfred Stieglitz—the whole "modern movement" in the arts. I suddenly saw the outlines of a book which would begin with the rise of the realistic novel after the Civil War and go up to the thirties, tracing the emergence and celebration in American literature of a very necessary historical spirit—the spirit, for example, that was expressed by the great radical critic Randolph Bourne when he conceived of America as a place of enormous Whitmanesque hope. And I began the book very much the way one might begin a novel of the past, with William Dean Howells arriving in New York, giving up his Boston career, and so on. On the other hand, I didn't think that

---

Another in the HORIZON interview series
THE ARTIST SPEAKS FOR HIMSELF
under the editorship of George Plimpton

I was writing anything but criticism.

INTERVIEWER: How did you actually set about writing the book?

KAZIN: Well, I remember starting it the day after I was first married, in 1938. There was a definite connection in my mind.

INTERVIEWER: What sort of connection?

KAZIN: I felt very liberated, very happy. I felt all sorts of things about the future. I felt I could really get to work now on a book of my own. And I did. The book was finished in 1942, so I worked on it for over four very active years. I would open the New York Public Library in the morning—the third-floor reading room, 315—and sometimes I would close it in the evening. I must say I was completely engrossed. I taught at City College and the New School at night, and wrote occasional reviews. We lived very modestly, and writing the book was certainly a gamble on my part. When the book came out and the reviews were so laudatory, I was quite astonished.

INTERVIEWER: Why, exactly?

KAZIN: What was astonishing to me was the sense I got from the reviewers that, working quite by myself, I had done a cultural history of an age that was passing. For by that time we were well into the war and had seen the Soviet-Nazi alliance come and go, and it was just beginning to be clear that the leftist idealism of the book, and its grand historical design, expressed the confidence of a period that had ended. Now it has become altogether clear.

INTERVIEWER: But nevertheless the book goes on?

KAZIN: Yes, it's having a second or third life in the universities despite the uneasiness of many professors. I was amused to read a critical symposium the other day in which a Yale professor criticized the book as too "democratic" in its prejudices, unfair to Henry James and Faulkner, and so on. It never occurred to him that it was precisely the "democratic" and radical passion of the book that has kept it alive. I was writing about my own period, and the book does represent the spirit of the time.

INTERVIEWER: But a lot of writers must have felt confidence in the hopeful possibilities of the thirties, and they didn't undertake a full-scale literary history. Where does the critic find such confidence of judgment?

KAZIN: It seems to me that a critic like myself is always more positive than he knows himself to be. Every critic who's worth a damn is always more than the man he seems. To be a critic, to be a good critic, is not simply a matter of having special taste. It's a matter of having a very strong point of view which is joined to the sense of the book at hand. I've always had an ability to enjoy a book, even to be moved to tears by it, and yet to be objective about it and judge it as I go along. As for what "judgment" is, God only knows. I can't say how I get it, but again and again I'm struck by the fact that I'm shocked by works of art, movies, statues, pictures, and books which intelligent people go ga-ga over and which seem to me absolute rot, because it's quite clear to me that there has been something insincere and undynamic in the creation.

INTERVIEWER: I wonder about the confidence it must take to revise judgments. The essays in *The Inmost Leaf* and in your new book *Contemporaries* show that your views have changed considerably since *On Native Grounds*.

KAZIN: Yes, of course many of my views have changed. Not only was my judgment more tentative then, my experience of life was more limited. And in fact I was sometimes more timid about trusting my own ideas than I should have been. For instance, I *did* feel at the time that Howells was pretty thin gruel, but I tended to be rather too pious about his social importance. Howells now seems to me a pleasantly gifted but in many ways disheartening writer because of his fear of basic human conflicts. And I badly underestimated Faulkner. Certainly my fundamental error, though, was in conceiving the book on a purely national scale, neglecting the larger European perspective. I wrongly assumed that the thirties—my own

period, so to speak—was a natural continuation of the high American creative period in the twenties, and that a great historical future lay before us in which the radical and artistic temperament would flourish.

INTERVIEWER: How do you view the thirties now?

KAZIN: Well, if you look back at the writing of the thirties now, you'll find two quite different periods. There were some great and wonderful books written up to, say, 1934 or 1935, and these were still very much in the independent spirit of the twenties. Scott Fitzgerald's *Tender Is The Night* is an example. But after 1935—interestingly enough, the time when the Popular Front began—American writers tended to lose their sharp edge. Far from being the basis for a forward movement in the arts, the great American writing of the twenties really marked the end of a long era.

INTERVIEWER: What do you mean by that?

KAZIN: I mean that the twenties marked the apex, the culmination, of the trend of bourgeois freedom that began with the French Revolution and really died with the First World War. The giants of modern European literature—Joyce, Proust, Yeats, and so on—could only have come out of that prewar freedom. American writers were still able to absorb that spirit to a certain extent through the twenties, but by the 1930's the Western world, to put it oversimply, was getting more and more flattened out, more organized into the mass society of our day. We saw writers like Hart Crane, D. H. Lawrence, and Mayakovsky—writers still possessed by what the romantics called "vision"—dying, often by their own hands. In Russia we saw gifted writers like Babel and Yessenin forcibly shut up. We saw Trotsky, one of the last true Russian intellectuals still in power, going off into exile and the state becoming cruelly harnessed to the brutal paranoia of Stalin. And then came the totalitarian state in Germany. The historical ideals and possibilities that survived into the twenties were evaporating. In the mid-

thirties, in fact, we actually saw extremely gifted writers being sympathetic to totalitarianism.

INTERVIEWER: Who, for example?

KAZIN: The most dramatic one, perhaps, is Louis-Ferdinand Céline, the French novelist who became pro-fascist, and who to my mind is in many ways the most striking figure in French writing after Proust. Just as Proust's work embodies an ultimate faith in human values, so Céline expresses the snarling desperation of the gifted writer who finds himself stuck, unable to believe in *any* of the traditional hopes for man. And after Céline, the protagonist in European fiction is often conceived not as a rebel or a revolutionary, but as the Stranger—the passive victim who is entirely indifferent to public values. By the "Stranger" I don't mean the hero of Camus's wonderful little book so much as I do the inarticulate, unconsciously suffering nihilist of so many hipster American works—the man who suffers from not knowing what to believe in, and who defends himself in the frivolous fashion of our society by pretending that there is nothing to believe in. What has happened is that the age is now working *against* the writer in a peculiarly destructive way—the way that destroyed Mayakovsky—and not *with* the writer as I had imagined and hoped when I was writing *On Native Grounds*. I must add, though, that I've continued to have the strongest identification with my old ideals. The independent tradition of American radicalism and protestant thought running from Emerson to Whitman to the Faulkner who wrote *A Fable* means more to me than ever. But I take a much chastened view of making those hopes real, and of the writer acting as their creative agent.

INTERVIEWER: You think, then, that there is a totalitarian threat to the artist in this country comparable to the one you've described abroad?

KAZIN: I certainly do. It is occurring more subtly and doesn't yet seem so acute and disastrous. But there has been the same collapse of ideals and along with it a gradual diminishing of intellectual freedom and speculation. For example, before the First World War it was fairly common for historians to attack the Constitution as an expression of class interests. Today such an attack would seem blasphemous. The sense that we must *necessarily* support the established system gets more demanding. And one ugly sign of this is the way public expression of all sorts has become so concerned with creating "images"—with contriving a persuasive effect on people, not in stating or searching out the truth. There's been an incredible production of false and ready-made language that may have been softening us up for totalitarianism.

INTERVIEWER: What is the effect of this in the arts today?

KAZIN: The whole thing might be illustrated, I think, by the way pure form has been divorced from meaning in the arts and in communication generally. The artistic revolutions before and after the First World War made endless experiments with form—the cubists and modern poets, the twelve-tone musicians, and so on. But they genuinely felt the need of new forms to express new perceptions. Today one sees all sorts of apparently advanced artistic forms—cubist and surrealist techniques —taken over wholesale by the ad agencies, who use them simply as tricks to persuade.

Back in the twenties when e.e. cummings started using his lower-case style and typographical squiggles, it seemed clear enough that he *needed* to express himself in that way. It was another New England poet's revolt against the genteel tradition. But if you read some of the poems coming out today in the really bad Beat magazines—poems glorifying violent sex—you realize that these writers aren't thinking of what they're saying so much as *how it affects the reader.* I'd sum up the difference by saying that the great writers of the age that ended in the twenties believed they could freely get access to the truth: the great writer was an evangelist of the *undisclosed* truth. But in our time, it's be-

come a question of how to get to *work* on people, of making self-conscious gestures. One has only to think of the differences between Faulkner and, say, Tennessee Williams.

INTERVIEWER: Do you now see Faulkner in that way—as one of the evangelists out of the twenties?

KAZIN: Certainly. He is a particularly good case to take because he's so different from the newer Southern writers. Faulkner now seems to me a moving example of a man with an almost religious trust in the power of truth to carry him on his way as a writer. He expresses the agony of an upper-class Southerner lamenting the loss of a tradition which came to an end with the Civil War. But his compassion for the Negro in the *Light in August* or for Dilsey in *The Sound and the Fury* goes deep into the eternal pathos of the individual struggling against death to "have his say," as Faulkner puts it. So Faulkner is far more than a good writer using Southern material. He manages to sum up a whole tradition, as Whitman sums up the last of romantic, expansionist, confident America. He seems to me, in fact, the last American writer of great vision— the last in the tradition of Emerson or Whitman or Melville, the last writer who said to himself, "I am the axis on which the universe turns." And that is why Faulkner looks so marvelously independent.

Now take a postwar Southern writer like Tennessee Williams: he is certainly gifted, but we see in him a typically contemporary — and minute — concern with the neurotic private problems of yearning people no longer in conflict with a hostile commercial society. Although he has written fiction, he prefers to work directly as a playwright: perhaps there's some need for immediate adulation, immediate applause. In any case, I find the same intent in his work that I find in so many other postwar writers: I feel he'll do anything, tear off anybody's clothes, to get a *frisson* out of the audience. Faulkner simply doesn't think in that manipulative way.

INTERVIEWER: It would seem that

you're pretty disheartened about postwar writers.

KAZIN: If I sound that way, I must make it clear that I don't feel so. Our times do present extraordinary difficulties for the writer, but I know of many writers today whom I admire enormously. In fact, I think there are more gifted writers today than ever before in America. And when I read novelists like Saul Bellow, Bernard Malamud, James Jones, Norman Mailer, and James Baldwin, or a critic like Harold Rosenberg, or a poet like Robert Lowell, I feel I'm in contact with minds that are open and implacable—minds that want to get to the bottom of things.

INTERVIEWER: Would you single out a postwar novel that you admire?

KAZIN: Well, I thought James Jones's novel *From Here to Eternity* was very strong, a book of extraordinary power. Jones wasn't just passing through the Army like Kilroy. He knew it. I was appalled by the snobbery of people who concluded that because it was a best seller it must somehow have been cheap, for it stands quite above most of the other war books. Much as I like Norman Mailer's later work, I can't now read *The Naked and the Dead* at all. I find it a literary concoction. What struck me most in Jones's book was the loneliness of Prewitt. He seemed to me a more positive and genuinely tragic version of the peculiarly contemporary character I talked about earlier: he's the Stranger in great danger of being run down by organized society, who has great trouble just staying alive, and who yet manages to hold on to some sense of justice, of reverence for life. There are other things I enjoyed in Jones's book—his grasp of the Army both as an authoritarian machine and as a vocation, for example—but one thing I admired particularly was his way of dealing with sex. I am appalled in contemporary literature by the way frustrated revolutionaries and rebels like Norman Mailer have made an ideology of sex. Sex is sex, not politics. When Jones describes a soldier shacking up with a half-breed girl, he shows the kind of arrangements that are in fact made with "Army" girls; he succeeds in putting sex into natural terms.

Those are some of the reasons I enjoyed *From Here to Eternity* so much. Jones is primarily concerned with narrative, as a true novelist must be; but he's immersed himself in the grain of a complex social world, and there is not too much "big thinking" in the book to be in excess of the story. So I think it stands along with other good American social novels. And the novel of society, as written by such masters as Dreiser and Dos Passos, seems to me the strongest form we have.

INTERVIEWER: And yet it seems to be the rarest form of fiction being written at the moment.

KAZIN: Yes. One reason may be this: we may seem externally to be much alike in America, but we are really very split up by regions, race, and class. We don't all speak the same language. And our finest social novels, like those of Faulkner and the best of Dos Passos, have been quite specialized—and extremely knowing—studies of vivid and distinct worlds. Now this seems to be harder and harder for the novelist to do. When James Gould Cozzens, for example, talks so abstractly about small-town love in *By Love Possessed,* it means much less to me than the marvelous, hard detail in his *Guard of Honor.* I used to see Cozzens in the Pentagon during the war when he was aide to a general, and I used to think, "He's a spy taking endless notes."

INTERVIEWER: Do you mean that American life has become so homogenized that it is hard for novelists to find and know distinctive worlds to write about?

KAZIN: No, I really don't think that, but I'm aware that some young writers do. Years ago writers did seem much more conscious of themselves as part of a race, a clan, a place, they could write about. It's interesting, you know, to ask why one region in America suddenly becomes a literary center and then goes down. Before the Civil War the literary center was New England. Then, from the 1880's to the early twenties, practically all the most important American novelists came from the Middle West: Willa Cather from Nebraska, Sherwood Anderson from Ohio, Theodore Dreiser from Indiana, Ernest Hemingway from Oak Park, Illinois, Scott Fitzgerald from Minnesota, John Dos Passos from Chicago. Who are the novelists from the Middle West today?

INTERVIEWER: Well, Saul Bellow.

KAZIN: Yes, Bellow was born in Canada but he did grow up in Chicago, and Chicago, in fact, has traditionally been a fine town for writers; it's big enough to be exciting, but not so big as to make the individual feel hopelessly small. New York seems to swallow writers up. I know of no good book about New York as a whole—nothing as good as *The Bostonians* by Henry James, or the ones on Chicago by Dreiser and Saul Bellow. My point, though, is that there are very few writers from the Middle West today.

INTERVIEWER: How do you explain this?

KAZIN: It seems to me that the Middle Westerners could *once* feel that they came from a region that was culturally intact and also had a tradition which in some way challenged the eastern plutocracy. You remember Fitzgerald's passages at the end of *The Great Gatsby* about the corrupt world of the East. But then in the thirties there was another shift and we had the rise of a very gifted group of Southern writers—James Agee, Robert Penn Warren, Eudora Welty, and so on. And here again we're aware of writers coming out of the province into the greater world—and of the province itself being corrupted and invaded.

INTERVIEWER: Perhaps there are fewer and fewer provinces today.

KAZIN: Perhaps, in the traditional sense. There's less of the feeling that Fitzgerald had when he was in New York—making a lot of money writing for *The Saturday Evening Post,* being married to Zelda, everything else—but never losing the sense that he was a naïve kid from Minnesota who was privileged just to be at the Plaza, for whom the world of the twenties was exciting and delicious. In a way we don't get that original provincial sense any more. But still it is impossible not to be struck by the number of writers who have come from minority groups since the thirties: the Jewish writers like Bellow, Bernard Malamud, Norman Mailer, Herbert Gold, J. D. Salinger—and how many others?—and the Negro writers like James Baldwin and Ralph Ellison. Their power seems to be channeled by their sense of apartness, of the specific experiences behind them. This doesn't mean, of course, that they should be lumped together. I couldn't be more aware of how different they are. For instance, in a novel like *The Assistant,* Malamud writes with a marvelous pure contemplation of the experience in the story—out of respect for the people themselves. He avoids the endless psychological probing that makes the work of a brilliant writer like Salinger nevertheless shaky to me. The writer who interests me is the writer who in some way has his eye on the object, who is absolutely fascinated by something outside of himself, whereas the nonwriter, the would-be writer, the slick writer, and all the innumerable sophisticates are driving us crazy by their awareness of themselves creating.

INTERVIEWER: I gather you know some of these writers personally. Does this affect your view of their work?

KAZIN: Knowing a writer well doesn't affect my judgment of his book—at least I hope it doesn't—but it certainly can affect my freedom to publish that judgment. It's not easy to write a harsh review of a friend, and often enough when I cannot praise a friend I am silent. Still, since most of my friends *are* writers, and are pleasing to me because they have the supple and sensitive minds that writers can have, I may on occasion find a relationship ending because of a bad book (a book *I* thought was bad) that began because of a good book (a book *I* thought was good). But whatever the reticences and courtesies that life calls for, a critic should never falsify his own judgment. In many ways that's all he has; the strength of his vocation lies in that.

INTERVIEWER: I wonder about the actual process of your own writing. How do you go about it?

KAZIN: I conceive of every piece as an essay, an exploration of my thought on the subject. I assemble my materials very systematically, then write my first drafts very fast, in order to meet the subject head on, to seize all its necessary implications.

INTERVIEWER: How do you mean, systematically?

KAZIN: Well, when I read a book, I mark passages. Then I go back, reread these passages, type them all out, and study them. At the same time I note down the ideas that occur to me while reading. This note-taking may go on over a period of days or weeks, and I keep the typed notes in a loose-leaf folder so I can get my texts easily. But then when I sit down to write, the actual composition is an amazingly unconscious process. I try to follow an inner line of thought. Whenever this thread breaks, I know I'm going wrong. But if I feel it's going right, I continue on to the end and often write ten or fifteen pages of first draft in one day. Later on, I may have to work for weeks to make the thing readable and publishable. It used to take me three drafts to complete an essay, but now I've gotten it down to two.

INTERVIEWER: Did you find yourself using a similar method for *A Walker in the City,* your autobiographical book about childhood in Brooklyn?

KAZIN: Very much so. *A Walker in the City* grew out of a personal notebook, which I've been keeping steadily since 1938 and which is my great resource as a writer. I write in it almost every day, and now I've collected perhaps twenty-five or thirty loose-leaf books. In the early forties I tried using some of this material in a novel, but it bored me. Then I set out to write a new kind of autobiography based on New York as my personal landscape. As I got it down to essentials—the final version, published in 1951, was one eighth

of the original manuscript—I knew that I'd found my kind of book.

INTERVIEWER: In what sense?

KAZIN: It shook me up completely, writing that book. It gave me a direct and firsthand feel for concrete images and felt phrases, and my style changed, and also my view of literature itself. My essays on romanticism, on *Moby Dick,* on my edition of Emerson—the ideas in them all grew as I worked on the *Walker* and wrote in my notebooks. The notebook itself is a travel report into my thought and experiences—there are notes on people, books, travel, etc.—but essentially it's an exercise in getting at my thought about anything and everything. Once I know what I really *think* about anything, I'm on my way.

INTERVIEWER: And you're working on a second autobiographical book now?

KAZIN: Yes. It's the kind of book that means more to me than almost anything else I do. I've taught in colleges and universities, but I've never regarded myself as a professional scholar or formal academic critic. I've tried to work out a career as an independent man of letters. And that is a hard stance for a critic to take in America, and one not easily accepted.

INTERVIEWER: Why is this so?

KAZIN: In countries with a deep, long, and *unconscious* sense of tradition, the philosopher or historian or critic may be regarded as a man of letters—if he functions as one. But our idea of literature seems now to be confined to novels and poetry. Apparently any first novel about losing one's virginity is more "creative" than *The Education of Henry Adams* or Edmund Wilson's *To the Finland Station* or, for that matter, the seminal books by Emerson, Thoreau, Parkman, John Jay Chapman, and so on. This is rot, but it is the cultural atmosphere in which I have to write and publish. Though I've earned my living as a professor and journalist, I've done so in order to support myself as a *writer*. I don't think much of American magazines in general—they look to me like rather tired department stores. But I need them, and not just economically.

Articles are essential to me as a writer. And I've never published anything I consciously thought unsatisfactory.

INTERVIEWER: How do you regard the present generation of literary critics?

KAZIN: It seems clear to me that those of us who started in the twenties and thirties had a certain advantage. We came in at a time when it still seemed natural to relate literature and the arts to history, to the traditional past and the necessary future. When I wrote *On Native Grounds,* I was aware of having a great tradition to call on. Today, in contrast, it seems natural for many students of literature not to have positive opinions. There is a pervasive uncertainty that finds a home in the university and in safe specialties. One has little sense of large concerns. But criticism is nothing if it's not the sense of large concerns brought urgently to bear on some particular text. The more interesting the critic, the more he's likely to know his own mind. This is essential. He's a carrier of value, not a mechanical analyst of "beauty." As Santayana said years ago, it's always a critic's values that make him interesting. He gets people to see the enormous moral universe implicit in a particular book or poem. But to operate this way, you must be a conscious carrier of tradition—not of the formal specific tradition, but of the values and strivings associated with it. That is why, when you read the work of the interesting people in American criticism today—Edmund Wilson, Lionel Trilling, Harold Rosenberg, or Erich Heller—you always find a concern with tradition in the broadest sense. In the end, tradition is what makes a critic, the tradition he grows out of and the tradition he tries to re-establish independently, for its inherent meaning. And when there is a break in tradition —too injurious a sense of "strangeness" —the critic wants to restore consciousness of it. The ancient gods are still there, waiting to be recognized.

Robert B. Silvers is an editor of Harper's *and* The Paris Review, *and was joint editor of* Writing in America.

O
RARE
HOFFNUNG

From 1939 to 1959 there lived in England an unconventional man named Gerard Hoffnung. For a cartoonist with a penchant for social satire to be an original fellow is not unusual in itself, nor is the fact that he was something of a professional clown. But as a satirist he had one great distinguishing weakness: he was not a mean man. For a biting social critic this is not only unconventional, it is downright foolhardy. To draw dowagers (as Hoffnung does opposite) who are ridiculous but rather pleasant is to willfully disarm oneself. To show a gouty old codger who is clearly harmless is to squander an opportunity. To compensate for this generosity Hoffnung elevated the little people. Animals, short balding men, fat old ladies, and cleaning women could be sure of more than an even break from Hoffnung. (One of his favorite models was his own cleaning woman, shown overleaf in her bath: with all the aplomb of a leader of society, she is drawing a cup of tea from what is in England the typical rusty water-heater.)

Hoffnung protagonists are easy to recognize: they have gentle, almost simple smiles, round chins, rounder noses, and an air of sweet repose. When the calm of a Hoffnung has been ruffled, he wears an air of startled surprise, nonplused but at the same time resigned—this is the way of the world, and he knows it. The case of the inflated lady on page 107 is a case in point.

The man Hoffnung was a Hoffnung only on the outside. Although he resembled a kind of Teutonic Pickwick and his mien was deceptively mild, inside he was like a lion. Soon after his career as an artist was launched, he turned to music, taking up the ocarina and then, with a sense that it was made for him, the tuba. He had always been a high-frequency whistler: now he painstakingly learned to read notes so he would know when to *oompah*. He practiced the tuba at all times but often at midnight, sometimes in Alpine shorts, and usually on stairs because, he said, the acoustics were better there. He took little interest in music that antedated Berlioz because the tuba parts were thin or non-existent. His most memorable coup was a gigantic musical spoof staged in London in 1956, "The Hoffnung Interplanetary Music Festival"; its sequel was presented in 1958. For these extravaganzas Hoffnung enlisted the services of such people as Aaron Copland and Dame Edith Evans, and commissioned scores like *The Tales of Hoffnung,* an "opera" in which the Valkyrie appeared astride Lambrettas. He needed the motor scooters, Hoffnung said, for the full bass sound.

During Gerard Hoffnung's brief lifetime (he died suddenly at the age of thirty-four) his cartoons appeared frequently in British periodicals such as *Punch* and *Lilliput*. Those on these pages will appear this fall in a book, *Ho Ho Hoffnung*, published by Harper & Brothers. Hoffnung also turned out a small shelf of cartoon books about music, illustrated Colette's setting of Ravel's *L'Enfant et les Sortilèges*, and made a series of "spontaneous unrehearsed" television appearances that left a permanent mark on those whose fate it was to be connected with them. At the time of the Suez crisis he told one hapless producer that while they were on the air he meant to look straight into the camera and say, "Eden must go!" He sat before the microphone in the last few seconds, mouthing the words while the producer signaled frantically that he would be cut off if he dared. He didn't, of course.

ALL-OUT IN THE DESERT

Arabs. Wadis. T. E. Lawrence. Cameras.

Stars. Dollars. More dollars.

Can these elements be combined to make

the flawless film? A perfectionist

director is trying to find out—

pursuing either an ideal or a mirage

By JOHN KNOWLES

Few movies can have been as complicated to make as *Lawrence of Arabia*. It is being shot largely in the deserts of Jordan, which is about as far from the comforts of home as anyone can get, and is taking two, or perhaps three, or possibly four years to complete. It will dramatize and presumably explain satisfactorily the life of Colonel T. E. Lawrence, which was one of the most inexplicable of this century. The "extras" are Arab nomads, who are the last people to submit easily to Western supervision and order. And the director of all this conflict and confusion, David Lean, is trying to make a perfect film.

There are several reasons for such an ambition, the first being that David Lean is a perfectionist by nature. But there is also his reputation to be lived up to; his last movie was the critical and popular success *The Bridge on the River Kwai*. He was responsible for that striking combination of the lacy beauty of Venice and the Gothic angles of Katharine Hepburn called *Summertime*. He did cinematic justice to Charles Dickens in *Great Expectations*. He deepened and broadened a short Noël Coward play into *Brief Encounter*. A great deal is now expected of David Lean.

Then there is the money involved. Successful films today either cost next to nothing or huge fortunes. *Lawrence of Arabia* is to be a leading member of the second category. Millions and millions of dollars have already been spent; millions more will have to be spent to complete the film. All that money has been backing up behind the production like tons of water held behind a dam, a dam that David Lean has to construct out of the slim materials of legend, imagination, and taste.

He also has the responsibility of important stars to be done justice to: Sir Alec Guinness, Anthony Quinn, Anthony Quayle. He must also do justice to a twentieth-century classic, *Seven Pillars of Wisdom*, Lawrence of Arabia's account of his role in the Arab Revolt of 1916–1918, on which the film is based. Lawrence was a man playing for high stakes; so is David Lean.

The first quarter of *Lawrence of Arabia* was shot in South Jordan. Much of the time it was 125° F. in the shade. Food came by boat from Denmark. Aside from the work, there was little for the hundred Europeans in the company to do but complain. That they did. Around them frowned hundreds of Bedouins, the Arab nomads who consider all non-desert people inferior and decadent. The Bedouins lived in their tents in the desert, the Europeans stayed in an encampment beside the Gulf of Aqaba, and David Lean hung in symbolic isolation between them, living in a trailer surrounded by a few tents in the desert.

The last day of filming in South Jordan was very hot, cloudless, and windless. Shooting was to take place at a point ten miles inside a great Jordan valley called Wadi Rumm. The Europeans were flown in that morning, as usual, by DC-3 from Aqaba, a twenty-five-minute flight. Below them was the moon landscape of the desert, crimson in the morning light, forming a vast corridor of sand between two iron-red ridges of knobbed and turreted rock.

The plane came in and landed on the desert at the entrance to the Wadi. As the passengers got out they saw a large sheet of "water" in the distance, reflecting the mountains behind it. It was the local mirage, working as usual.

Strong morning sunshine poured down into a land where until now there had never been anything as loud as an airplane engine; where no fumes of Western civilization had ever penetrated—a place of indeterminate perspectives, interminable silences, and absolute clarity. Even this huge film operation, with its airplanes and fleets of vehicles and hoards of men and animals, was swallowed up and muffled and lost in all the silence and space.

Jeep engines erupted defiantly in the quietness, and the film company set off to drive, from where the airplane had landed, the ten spine-shaking miles into Wadi Rumm, following a bumpy track through sand striped in shades of pink and yellow and green, to a group of frail tents and wooden stables. Members of the Jordan Army cavalry who were being used in the film lived in the tents; their horses had more solid accommodations in the stables. The Jeeps continued over a rise and past more tents scattered with less order over the dunes; the Bedouins lived here with their camels, providing authentic extras for the movie by playing their own fathers and grandfathers, who had served with Lawrence during the Arab Revolt.

The Jeeps lurched on, driving past a small, neat, stone fort enclosed by barbed wire. A tall Arab in khaki-colored blouse and a skirt reaching to his ankles stood near the fort, cartridge belts across his chest, his head swathed in Arab headdress. "That'll photograph well," said a visitor to the film company, "but with the naked eye you can see that it's a little too perfect to be real." A member of the company said, "That is real. That's the Jordan Desert Patrol outpost."

Oh.

The Jeeps bumped on, rocking and pitching over and around big clumps of camel grass, swerving and swaying like little speedboats in a heavy sea. After a couple of miles of this they arrived at a tiny commotion in the vastness, a little wrinkle on the great face of the Wadi: the epic production-in-progress of *Lawrence of Arabia*.

Three bright little beach umbrellas shaded some camp chairs. There was a large camera truck and a large sound truck; there were more Jeeps. British technicians in shorts, with fair hair and blazing faces, loitered around the trucks; young Arab assistants in nondescript shirts and pants, but never shorts, idly chased lizards with sticks; European actors with dyed skin stood around in Bedouin robes; real Bedouins hovered in their own robes; an evil-faced Arab leaned down from his camel and said in clear Anglo-Saxon, "Eddie, it doesn't feel as though there's any foam rubber in this saddle to *me*"; and a figure in white hood and voluminous robes, also on the apex of a camel, loped off by himself. This was the movie's part-time Lawrence of Arabia, not the actor portraying Lawrence but the stand-in used for long shots. Like a mirror reflecting a reflection, this receding white figure, swaying on a camel, began to lose its actorish

109

Peter O'Toole as Lawrence of Arabia (left) follows his guide through a genuine Jordanian sandstorm

quality and to take on the appearance of Lawrence himself, a willful, a lone figure, moving toward a red slab of cliff.

Lean remained behind, alongside the camera truck. Until now he had been an inconspicuous member of the group there—a tall, thin, middle-aged man with a sensitive, harried face. He now coiled himself tensely into a camp chair and began to fume. The band of men and animals a mile away weren't in the exact position he wanted. "Move column nearer to us!" an assistant director said through a hand loudspeaker. His augmented voice went out like a siren across the sand and camel grass, and much later it echoed faintly back from a crevice in the cliff. Not one of the minute figures in the column seemed to hear. Again and again the direction shot out toward the cliff, bounced faintly back, and nothing happened. Finally a Jeep was sent to tell them what to do. It clambered and lurched through the desert

David Lean

and grass, a vague whirl of dust rising from its back wheels, and at last it crept up to the column. After a while the column began to move into the position Lean wanted. But then for some reason the Jeep did not withdraw. "Jeep, come back!" the assistant director bawled into his loudspeaker again and again. Nothing happened. David Lean climbed onto the roof of the camera truck, next to the camera itself, and kept repeating in his sharp Londoner's voice, "Get them out of there, tell them to come back." At length the Jeep began to make its slow, dusty way out of camera range. It jounced once more and then stopped, seeming to break down, to be stuck halfway between actors and camera.

"All right, everybody, quiet," said the assistant director into his loudspeaker.

"Shut up!" shouted David Lean without help.

There were one or two professional clicks and snaps, and then a gun was fired as a signal for the troop of mounted men to begin the scene. They set out, just perceptibly moving across in front of the huge dark-red slab of rock, a little tribe of insects inching along beneath the great wall of the valley. Around the camera truck, Lean and the cameramen and the assistant directors and the script girl and some Jordanian helpers stood motionless. There was no sound to be heard except a little scratching noise coming from the sound truck. Inside the large camera next to Lean, a few feet of film were being exposed.

In a minute or so it was finished. Most of the morning had been spent preparing for this scrap, but there was still time for a close-up of the same shot. Lean began with the women. They were playing Bedouin wives and were dressed in black accordingly, but they were not quite authentic. Bedouin women are not supposed to be photographed. So these city

Arab women had been brought from Jerusalem, and since they looked very much like the real thing they were the object of many doubts and suspicions on the part of the Bedouin men in the movie. They were arranged very interestingly, seated on top of a big rock outcropping.

But Lean was not entirely happy about their positioning. An Arab-speaking assistant went up onto the rock in the relentless sunshine, and Lean said through another assistant with a loudspeaker, "Will you ask the lady second from the right to move forward—yes, now back a little, just a bit, now will she sit down, no, the way she sat before, so that the red in her sleeves shows"—doubtfully—"y-e-e-s-s—and now will the other lady next to her . . ."

For half an hour the women on the rock were rearranged, and the small army of men on camels and horseback were held in readiness below them on the floor of the valley.

Then at last this shot too was ready.

"Quiet, please, everybody quiet," said the loudspeaker.

"Shut up!" shouted Lean.

The gun was fired and the large body of men on horses and camels started forward in a jumbled desert mass, the camels hung with blankets and tassels, their riders wearing their headcloths bandit-like across their mouths to filter the dust; and slightly higher than anyone, or so it seemed, Lawrence of Arabia, a hooded white figure hunched forward on his pitching camel. Above them the women rose and came forward to the edge of the rock, ululating—the Arab women's cry, a high, steady note broken by blocking the mouth quickly over and over with the hand.

It was this last detail that failed. From lack of practice or shyness the women didn't ululate enough to satisfy Lean. Back went the horses and camels, back to their original sitting position went the women on the rock, higher and hotter rose the sun, "Quiet please" and "Shut up!" broke the desert air again, and once more the camels and horses and riders and women converged toward the camera and Lean.

This time it would do. The umbrellas and chairs were swept up, the Jeeps started their engines, and everyone piled into them to drive back to the forward headquarters for lunch. Then everyone got into Jeeps again and bounced back to the new location, a little deeper into Wadi Rumm. Now there was a really long wait.

This was to be the last scene made in Jordan that year. Perhaps a year later the company would come back to do more of the still very large number of unshot Jordan scenes. Everything was far behind schedule. Large sections of the huge script (by the playwright Robert Bolt) were still being rewritten; scenes were being rehearsed and re-rehearsed, shot and reshot; a thousand details were slightly wrong; a thousand little snags were constantly developing; and above all there was the perfectionism of David Lean, which was turning *Lawrence of Arabia* into an unforeseen kind of epic.

It was certain to cost more than the Arab Revolt itself had cost; it was certain to take longer to film than it had taken Lawrence and the Arabs to break the Turkish Empire. European members of the company, including Lean himself, had been hurrying into hospitals in Jerusalem and Amman lately with some sudden complaint or other. One of the pilots had come in for a landing a few days before, with Anthony Quinn aboard, and had forgotten to lower his wheels. The desert was smooth, so only the plane was damaged.

Morale was low. The British technicians, used to all the protection and privilege of a welfare state, complained steadily about rights that were being denied them. The Bedouins alone were comfortable and accepted what came with steady desert resignation. But even they had their doubts. "They think we're balmy," said Peter O'Toole succinctly, one of the few who made an attempt to get to know them. It was appropriate that he should; he was playing Lawrence.

That afternoon preparations for the final scene, which was centered around him, went slowly forward. It all looked extremely effective—Lawrence in a soiled British World War I belted summer uniform, slumped exhausted on a rock; two desert sheiks in their robes, standing patriarchally over him; and on a hillside behind them the high-legged, high-nosed camels with robes in deep colors flung over their humps, their riders on foot, in robes and headcloths, and underfoot small, dark-colored rocks, thousands of them, growing more dramatic by the minute as the declining sun threw little shadows beside them. In the distance the great desert valley was also passing into the shadow of its far cliffs.

But there were a number of things that did not please David Lean. First of all, and crucially, the camera was pointed toward the west and had to be carefully angled so that the sun would not enter the lens and make photography itself impossible. A shield perhaps a foot square had to be held above the lens to make the shot possible. A rock outcropping near the parade of camels reflected too much light, so a man was dispatched to spray it a darker shade.

And then, what about the dialogue? It consisted of only four or five lines, but how were they to be said? Should Peter O'Toole be seated on the rock throughout the scene, or should he enter walking and then sink down in exhaustion? Lean rehearsed O'Toole doing it both ways. The veteran English actor John Ruddock, playing one of the sheiks, stood behind O'Toole. "This is the sun's anvil . . ." said Ruddock. But was standing the best position for him as he said this line? Lean had him sit.

"This is the sun's anvil . . ." he said again. Perhaps he should begin by sitting and then stand up as he said the line. And the other sheik, should he sit, stand, or do both? The three actors were told by Lean to try it in all possible combinations, one or more of them getting up or sitting down during the course of this minute scene. Which way was better, which way was best, which way was—for this was what Lean pursued—perfect?

"Where did you get those awful boots?" he suddenly asked O'Toole.

"I've been wearing them all along."

"Got that one past me," muttered Lean.

Finally all the decisions about camera angle, reflectors, the rocks, the robes, the camels, the desert floor, the actors,

their postures, the lines and how they were to be delivered, had been reached. The scene was ready to be put on film. For some last-second attention to his make-up O'Toole moved a few steps away from the camera and sat down on a stool. His make-up man quickly sprayed some dust on his uniform and began giving him some extra sweat. Lean suddenly loomed over him, muttering breathlessly, "Hurry up! Hurry up!" With his loose, light summer clothes flapping on his tall thin frame, he jerked across the rock, consciously clamping control on his nerves. "We haven't much time!" he said in this same electric undertone. "Hurry!"

O'Toole took a last look at his long, regular-featured, slightly wayward-looking, sun-tanned face in a mirror, at his yellow-dyed hair, and stood up. He stepped in front of the camera and sank exhausted on the rock. Behind him the sheik began his line, "This is the sun's anvil . . ."

"Stop," said Lean quietly. "I'm sorry, it's too late." The sun had entered the camera; the scene was unfilmable.

O'Toole let fall one short, passionate obscenity. "I'm sorry," he said, "I'm sorry." Because the extra attention to his make-up had caused the final delay, he seemed to conclude that the failure was due to him. He had forgotten that it was Lean who had rehearsed the scene to the point where the slightest delay would undo it.

The director stood amid the wrecked scene alone for a moment, wearing the look of tense pleasure certain sensitive faces wear when absorbing a deep disappointment.

And then everything began to be folded and packed with the practical haste of, say, a group of Arab nomads, the camera and umbrellas and stools and kits, the paint, the light reflectors—into the trucks and Jeeps it all went, followed by the technicians, the actors, and the director. Like an army in disorderly retreat after a bad defeat they jounced and careened away down the desert valley, and not far behind them the Bedouins in their hundreds swayed along on their camels with much more composure. Few, if any, knew what had happened or why. They knew they would get their final pay, that this unusual form of labor was over.

But for the *Lawrence of Arabia* company it was the end, on a very sour note, of filming in Jordan. The machinery that had brought and sustained them here was already well advanced in the process of carrying them out again. They bounced down Wadi Rumm and into the airplanes, away to Aqaba, to Amman, to Beirut, to London, for some interior shots; then they would go to Spain; and then, perhaps next year, they would come back to Jordan. They were, in fact, nomads, the most expensive ever, because what they were seeking was perfection. But everyone knows how careless about everything except essentials true nomads are.

Author of two novels, Morning in Antibes *and* A Separate Peace *(which won three literary awards, including the first ever given by the William Faulkner Foundation)*, John Knowles *has traveled widely through the Middle East.*

A European traveler strikes across two contrasting countries and cultures and discovers when

Where Kursk and Kansas Meet

The Englishman Mervyn Jones, a reporter for the London Observer *and a rising author in the field of sociology (an area that also engaged his father, the late Dr. Ernest Jones, the biographer of Sigmund Freud) recently made extensive comparative tours of both the United States and the Soviet Union. What he has found, from the point of view of a visiting explorer of the highways and low-ways of both nations, will form part of his book* The Antagonists, *to be published in the fall by Clarkson N. Potter, Inc.*

The road is weak against the strength of the land. It marks a line, straight and hard, over the soft strangeness; but *over* it, and not *in* it, like the hedged and sunken roads I know at home in England. This is America, or this is Russia. They differ, as I shall be saying, in an infinity of matters; but in their size they are alike. And size, as the traveler covers mile after mile, is the most powerful of facts, the most indelible of impressions.

Sometimes the landscape is monotonous, sometimes simply repetitive. The truly monotonous landscape is the open plain, flat as a table, whose immense fields of wheat or Indian corn are laid out by geometry. This is fearsome country, denying the sense of movement, reducing the car or the train to an insect laboring across a lawn. Iowa is like this, and the southern Ukraine. Yet it is not the plain that gives the most overpowering sense of vastness. One knows that it is only a part of America, or of Russia; an unusual part, in which plainsmen, like mountaineers, find a special quality.

The repetitive landscape is more ordinary, and there is more of it. The pattern runs, commonly, for five miles. Fields cover the flank of a long, gentle descent. They are interrupted once or twice by woods, or by something less definable than a wood—by brush, by undergrowth, by a straggle of bushes and briars. A bridge, making no rise in the road, crosses a small and sluggish creek. Hereabout there is a village or a small town. More fields, more brush. Then the road, still straight, mounts the incline of another whaleback hill. The crest is reached unremarked, and the pattern begins again.

One may have seen what I have described, or one may—chatting or reading or asleep—have missed seeing it. One has in any case seen it dozens of times. With a jolt of the

imagination one realizes that it is a named segment of the huge country, a segment within whose invisible boundaries people remain for weeks together and indeed live their whole lives. And the countless number of these segments makes up the vastness. This unending nothing-in-particular—neither flat nor hilly, neither beautiful nor ugly, neither crowded nor empty—is America all the way from western Pennsylvania out to Colorado. It is Russia all the way from Leningrad down to Kiev, and (so they tell me) all the way from Poland to the Urals.

I went to America and to Russia in 1961 (the former for the first time after a fourteen-year interval, the latter for the first time in my life) because to know these countries is essential to a knowledge of the modern world. If you come from northwestern Europe, nothing brings home the size of these great countries as much as the amount of land that is not used. There is no English word for what Americans call "brush." Americans traveling in England remark on its absence; they can find only fields, and woods carefully maintained for timber. Their surprise is matched by that of the Englishman who adds up—saying nothing, of course, of the real desert or the big mountains—the square miles in America that are neither farms, nor productive forests, nor golf courses, but are simply left alone.

Throughout America, even in what are thought of as the agricultural states, you come across stretches of wilderness. In such a big country, I suppose, a few score square miles here and there don't matter. If the United States were to split up into a number of small nations, each on bad terms with its neighbors and striving to be self-sufficient, the food production of the continent would increase by leaps and bounds. Rocks would be yanked out, scanty soil irrigated, swamps drained, hillsides terraced as in frugal Italy. But America, big America, can pick and choose. Her problem is in fact to dispose of all the food that does get grown.

In Russia, too, the psychology of the big country is dominant. It is thought simpler, evidently, to open up a vast tract of virgin land in Kazakhstan than to deal with that difficult patch a few miles from Novgorod—even though the latter can be multiplied over and again. Especially in the northern part of the country, brush is greatly in evidence.

The soil, certainly, is thin and inclined to be sandy. Still it is much the same across the border in Finland, and there far more of it is under the plow.

Aside from the size of the land, what is bound to impress any visitor to Russia is the scope and vigor of the housing program. "A flat for every family by 1980" is surely, to the average Russian, the most important of the promises in the Party program. From my observation it is a promise that is pretty sure to be kept. In some towns the authorities told me that the target would be reached well ahead of time, and the present rate of construction justifies the forecast. Russia is moving, therefore, toward a very notable achievement. If matters don't improve, there will still be waiting lists in France and England, and slums in America, in 1980; and the contrast to be foreseen is likely to have an even greater impact than the contrast on the industrial scene between the first Five Year Plan and the Depression.

There is a great deal of new building in evidence everywhere. Cranes and scaffolding sprout like liana vines in the tropics; cement dust fills the air; whole districts become impenetrable while an onslaught is launched as though on a besieged city. When a street is roped off and traffic diverted, it is not because the roadway is being repaired, but because all the buildings are being demolished and replaced. It is no exaggeration to say that Moscow is one vast building site. Except as a result of war damage, there can never have been such an example of a whole city being rebuilt on the spot.

The now accepted version of Soviet history depicts the later years of Stalin's rule as a degeneration or caricature of the earlier. This is emphatically true in the field I am discussing. Whether or not the priorities were right, what got built in the earlier phase was socially useful. What got built later was no use to anyone except to house the bureaucracy or to feed a pathetic megalomania.

Most people have seen pictures of the twenty- and thirty-story "wedding-cake" buildings of Moscow—especially of the University, the most elaborately ghastly of all—but on first coming face to face with one of them, the visitor's immediate reaction is surely that it can't really be true. Recovering a little, he may reflect that it has at least one purpose: he can orient himself by it, as by the Eiffel Tower as one goes about Paris. If he does so, he soon becomes bushed,

like the wanderer in the jungle coming repeatedly upon the same—or is it the same?—gigantic cotton tree. There are in fact no fewer than seven of the things, not counting the University—which can be distinguished, though never escaped, because it stands on a hill toward the fringe of the city.

I am not sure what all seven contain, but most of them provide spacious homes for the Ministry of This, the Institute of That, and the Headquarters of the Other. If we imagine that during the headlong growth of Washington in recent years no slums were cleared, no new houses built, and everything sacrificed to the creation of the Pentagon, we can have some notion of the resentment that the most loyal Muscovite must have felt as yet another of these latter-day Great Pyramids cast its shadow on his humble home. When Stalin died, his successors knew that something had to be done about housing, and fast.

Now if a British dictator pledged himself to the manufacture of a hundred million cars, he would be interested neither in the unusual design of the MG nor in the superb craftsmanship of the Rolls-Royce. He would probably begin by closing down both the MG and the Rolls-Royce factories. This is what Khrushchev is doing to get his houses.

If you stand on the Dnieper Bridge, with the city of Kiev behind you on the right bank of the river, and look at what is virtually a new town growing like ripe corn on the left bank, and if you try to count the blocks of flats that stand in a line as straight as geometry on the vast plain, then you will soon lose count. There are a great many blocks, and they are all alike: the same height, the same length, the same color and appearance. From the air, one might be looking down on a row of matchboxes arranged by an obsessional child. And not only this, but the blocks are exactly like other blocks outside Leningrad, and in Kishinev near the Rumanian border, and doubtless in Vladivostok.

A Russian architect, visiting London, was heard to explain with pardonable pride how he designed buildings to be put up in a remote Siberian town he had never visited. Architects do not all live in Moscow; Kharkov has forty. But, as the traveler can easily see, they cannot alter the master-design in any significant way; their main job is to fit it to the site. A medium-sized city, with two or three hundred

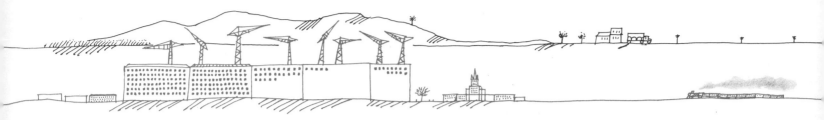

thousand people and a considerable housing program, has in most cases no architects at all but relies on the regional center. The reconstruction of Belgorod, for instance, was planned in Kharkov.

Every block that I saw anywhere in Russia had either forty, sixty, or eighty flats. The variation depended on the length, not on the height. The standard block has five stories, for one of the few immutable laws in force throughout both the Communist and the capitalist world is that you must put in a lift if you go up to six. One should not assume, however, that blocks of just the same shape will be put up from now to 1980. Moscow is evidently a testing ground where new ideas are tried out, and there I saw a group of slab blocks quite American in appearance and ten stories high. This is a mercy, for if Moscow were entirely rebuilt to the current designs, so that eight million people were living in identical five-story blocks, it would surely be the most appalling city on earth. Someone seems to have realized this.

The art of town planning is decidedly in abeyance. The blocks of flats stretch on and on, usually on either side of an enormously wide main road, at precisely regular intervals. The density of population is not terribly high (about 125 people to the acre); but the open space is provided in small regular chunks, mostly in the courtyards of the blocks, which does nothing to relieve the monotony. The idea of leaving a bit of countryside—say, a pleasant birch wood—between one group of blocks and the next has occurred to nobody. Building, it seems, is simply to go on and on, in space as well as in time, until there is enough. Urban sprawl, in fact, is just as characteristic of Russia as of any other country.

Russians love size with an unreflecting passion, and would be delighted if Moscow were the biggest city in the world. It is now, as they think, second only to New York—a belief that dramatizes the whole Russo-American contest. When I told them that Tokyo, according to the latest figures, is now the world's biggest city, the news that another metropolis had to be surpassed was obviously a jolt. Several people asked me to confirm that Moscow is now bigger than London. If I said they were about on a level, the polite rejoinder was "Moscow is a little ahead, I believe." If I then remarked that in my opinion both Moscow and London are too big, I was taken to be making an obscure joke.

In principle at least, urban renewal has nowhere been as badly needed as in America, where the decay of the city is far advanced. I ought to stress, however, that this decay is confined to the eastern half of the United States. For myself, although I could live in New York because it is a great city with unique qualities of its own, I should not willingly live in any other town east of the Mississippi; but I could reconcile myself to living in almost any town forward of the first rise into the Rockies. The difference between the East and the West is just as great now as when the former was in its heyday and the latter no more than a challenge to adventurers. It is a difference, I think, of which a traveler from Europe is more aware than an American. Europe has changed, since the war, more than the East of the United States. In the older American cities, because of the stale ugliness and the blatant poverty that wealth seems too weary rather than too callous to remedy, I felt myself taken back in time, felt a distinct odor of the 1930's. In the West, I felt tugged forward. In every way the place seems open to movement and to experiment. It cannot be accidental that there is more good modern architecture, and far more variety of style, in a small university town like Boulder, Colorado, than in all of New York—to say nothing of Philadelphia or Boston.

But the difference is not only to be marked in streets and buildings; you can sniff it in the air, hear it in voices, see it in the way people walk and in their faces. That there are vast new industries, new holiday centers, and towns where more than four inhabitants in five have come from somewhere else—this does not seem to me the most notable thing about the West. What strikes me above all is the tone in which people speak of these changes: a tone of wonder, more deeply felt, as well as much more attractive, than obvious pride. The West is the America that has not yet quite got used to itself, that retains the capacity for surprise. It occurs to me, too, that if there is any real similarity in atmosphere between America and Russia, it must be between the Mountain States and the Urals.

Nevertheless, there is one thing in common between the American cities that are decaying at the heart and those that are not, and this is a decided elephantiasis of the limbs. In

America, just as in Russia, very few people realize that the optimum and the maximum size of a city are not the same thing. The sheer length and breadth of an American city (if we disregard the official boundaries and think of the city as it really is) surely has no parallel on earth. Denver still has only 800,000 people, though it has doubled in the past decade; but it is eighteen miles across. The new missile plant, twelve miles out, employs 12,000 workers; and one might think that it would provide an obvious nucleus for a new town, separated from Denver by open country. But no: housing developments spring up on the edge of Denver (so that the missile workers can imagine they live "right in the city"), then sprawl farther out, and in a few years will doubtless cover the whole intervening space.

This is where they live, the Smiths and the Joneses and the Kellys and Cohens, the working-class and middle-class people who earn somewhere around the average American income. Once they lived in New York, Boston, or Chicago; and now they live in Greater New York, Greater Boston, or Greater Chicago. The monotony of the Russian blocks of flats is reflected in the monotony of the American suburbs. In England, heaven knows, there is monotony enough. But in England, after a not very great number of miles, the sprawl runs into another town or an old village or a pretty stretch of country whose preservation is respected. In Russia and in America it runs into nothing but more open country "suitable for development," and then more, and then more.

In America three factors maximize both the amount of land used and the impression of sameness. The civic authorities have lately been gripped by the idea of zoning—about the only form in which "planning" is acceptable. This means that a district where houses are built should contain nothing but houses. I came across a case in which a repair garage had been expelled, though in a community of car owners it surely seems as necessary as a laundry. With all places of employment banished to the industrial zone and all shops concentrated in the shopping center, even a street corner ceases to be a punctuation mark.

Then, every house has to have a garden. The purpose is not to grow food, as in Russia, nor to plant flower beds in a way expressive of some kind of individuality, as in England, but to have a lawn on which friends can be entertained in warm weather. All the gardens are the same size, because the lots were parceled out by the entrepreneur of the development, and with rare exceptions they all look alike.

The other factor is the curious reluctance of Americans to walk up stairs. This practice, surviving only in the older houses in the city proper, has become as obsolete as cranking a car. In the suburbs every house for miles is what English people call a bungalow. It is a simple square, the most uninteresting shape conceivable, and is known as a cracker-box, though in point of fact rather more thought and ornamentation would be devoted to a box of biscuits. This kind of house is surprisingly small. The amount of space in the three rooms and kitchen is less than in a prefab or a traditional two-story house in England, and not much more than in a Russian cottage. One wonders how the family finds room for the washing machine, the Deepfreeze, and all the rest of it; and this is only achieved by recourse to folding couches, gate-leg tables, bunk beds for the children, and such devices. One would suppose, too, that a man with a steady job at, say, $120 a week would make a down payment on something more commodious. But many Americans would rather have a car, a trailer, or a boat.

When an American does decide on a larger house, what he buys is more ground space. Instead of accepting the regulation lot, he negotiates for a "parcel of land" in what is still open country. Here he has a house built with six, eight, or ten rooms—still all on one floor—and with a bigger lawn. Soon, somebody else does the same on either side; the land is probably part of a former farm of several hundred acres bought up by a speculator. Thus the city sprawls.

The ultimate in this process, notably in the West, is the ranch-type house belonging to some millionaire. It has a vast glass-walled hall, a dozen bedrooms, as many bathrooms, a garage for four cars, and whatever else the architect can plausibly recommend, all without a staircase. This is an urban sprawl in itself.

"Private affluence and public squalor" is a phrase for which we are all grateful to Professor J. K. Galbraith, and which has passed into common usage because it expresses a truth about the world we live in. The second half of the

phrase, however, is more universally applicable than the first. Despite the lack of private affluence, there is a good deal of public squalor in Russia, and it often takes the same forms as in America. In both countries the streets are inadequately cleaned by the standards of western Europe (the reason why there is not much litter in Russia is that nobody has much to throw away, and the newspaper is kept to wrap the bread in). In New York, as in Moscow, there are public lavatories—not nearly enough of them, in either city—without doors to the cabinets and filled with a revolting stench. An equally powerful smell rises from rivers without proper embankments in both American and Russian cities when a spell of hot, dry weather exposes stretches of nauseous mud.

I don't know if one should be more shocked about this kind of thing in America, where there is national wealth and private affluence, or in Russia where the public weal is neglected in a professedly socialist society. What is equally saddening in both countries is the apparent rarity of complaint. It may be that in any very large nation the remoteness of authority promotes resignation. In any case, it is amazing what people will put up with.

Going along West Fifty-seventh Street in New York City, the bus started to pitch like a blunt-nosed cargo steamer in a rough sea. Passengers put away their newspapers as the print danced before their eyes; of those who had no seats, two or three lost their footing. In Russia, the surface of Fifty-seventh Street would be considered excellent. Moscow, well ahead of the rest of the country in this as in other respects, is the only city where asphalt surfaces are the rule and not the exception. Elsewhere, you find asphalt in a few central streets, such as the Nevsky Prospekt in Leningrad; cobbles in the other main streets; and earth, usually carved into deep ruts, in the rest.

In Russia I drove invariably on asphalt roads. The reason is that foreigners have to stick to an itinerary that is approved in advance, and only a small number of main highways are officially considered to exist. I wanted to return from Odessa to Lvov and thence to Warsaw, having heard from a Polish friend that there is a perfectly good road, but Intourist blandly maintained that there was no road at all.

As far as I know, only one road map of Russia is on sale in the West. It is published by a German firm, presumably from wartime knowledge. When I got there, I found myself driving on roads that took quite a different route from that marked on the map. By this time I had bought in Moscow an excellent road atlas, which marked the roads I was on and quite a number of others. Thus equipped, I resolved to take a few wrong turnings onto unauthorized roads, but at every fork I was deterred by the sight of two or three gimlet-eyed policemen, one of whom always had a motorcycle. I once turned into the ring road in the outskirts of Kiev, which connects with the unauthorized highway to Zhitomir; the police were after me like a shot.

Road accidents, like train crashes and air disasters, are never reported in Soviet newspapers—that would be regarded as sensationalism—nor are there any statistics on this matter. But, to judge by the dramatic warnings displayed on frequent billboards, the accident rate is causing the authorities some concern. The basic trouble is that the traffic, light though it seems to the visitor, has considerably increased in the past few years. Until lately the Russian driver could reckon on having the road to himself for as far as he could see. He still drives, therefore, as if he were alone in the Sahara, never giving a signal, looking in his mirror, or finding out if the road is clear before he makes a turn. He drives very fast, too. When Russians gather round a foreign car—and a crowd gathers as soon as you park, except in Moscow where people have become more blasé—they always ask about its speed, and almost never about its reliability or its gas consumption. My car has a top speed of about a hundred kilometers an hour; when I admitted this, I was invariably, promptly, and exultingly informed that a Russian car does 120. On the umpteenth occasion, slightly nettled, I retorted: "On these roads?" Nobody saw what I meant by the question.

Russian traffic regulations seem to contemplate a volume of traffic that, in spite of the increase, is still far from being a reality. In Moscow you are forbidden ever to turn left (you drive on the right, of course), and some right turns are also forbidden. Instead of turning left, you go on until you reach a point where a U-turn is allowed, return on your tracks, and turn right. In the wide avenues the traffic on the crown of the road is moving slowly or a file of vehicles is

stationary while waiting to U-turn. There is in any case no distinction between fast and slow lanes, and people pass on either side. It is also permitted to turn right against a red light, with the result that only those intending to turn right keep near the curb. If you obey the rules, you get involved in enormous detours.

Suppose you are in a side street on the north side of the Arbat—a shopping street quite near the center of Moscow—and want to get into a side street facing you on the south side. You have to turn right and drive west to the end of the Arbat, over a large square, down a hill, across a bridge, and into a highway leading out of the city. After a while you can make a U-turn, cross the river again, go up the hill, cross the square, go along the Arbat, and turn right. You will have covered a mile and a half instead of waiting for a gap in the traffic—which, at present volume, is sure to occur in a few minutes—and crossing the Arbat.

An even more baffling problem, which concerned me closely, is how to get from the National Hotel to the gasoline station near the Metropole, a distance that can be covered on foot in five minutes. As far as I could discover, there is no legal way of doing this whatever. My technique was to drive along Red Square, delve into some narrow streets that brought me to its far end (no U-turns in Red Square being allowed), come back along its entire length and, since by this maneuver I was on the side of the road near the petrol station, stop behind a policeman in order to make swiftly the forbidden right turn when he was not looking.

The rules are thus a formidable deterrent to driving in Moscow. My Russian guides, who were never car owners, were usually reduced to saying after we had gone round in circles for a while: "Well, I could get you there easily if we were not in a car."

The United States, under the program authorized by President Kennedy, presumably to get America moving again, and due for completion in 1972, is to build forty-one thousand miles of highways. This will cost forty-one billion dollars. One cannot help suspecting that some official, after wrestling with the estimates, said: "The hell with it, let's settle for a thousand bucks a mile—it's a good round figure." Be this as it may, the construction companies and the land speculators are looking forward to the greatest bonanza since the golden age of the railways.

The American highway program is essentially a monument to a past age, when the Boston executive, due to spend a couple of weeks with his mother on her ranch in Arizona, would immure his children in the back of the car with a supply of candy and comics, take turns at the wheel with his wife, cover seven hundred miles a day, and arrive with four days of his holiday gone and no zest for the remainder. Americans in the 1960's no longer behave like this; they fly and hire cars at the airport. Indeed, it always has been and doubtless always will be true that most road journeys are short and not cross-country. Few people really want to drive from New York to Chicago in less than fourteen hours, certainly not as many as would like to make the tortuous trip from Springfield, Massachusetts, to Providence, Rhode Island, in less than four. Besides, it is only in the main industrial regions that the American roads are really congested. Over most of the country the number of cars per mile of road—as distinct from the number per head of population—is much smaller than in Europe. A four-lane highway from Denver to Santa Fe is about as necessary as an airline over the North Pole. The attraction of the one, as of the other, is primarily romantic; the highway program is a kind of sputnik in concrete.

When writing about street surfaces, I recorded my impression that neither in America nor in Russia is there much care for the comfort or convenience of ordinary people. I was struck by this as a visitor; but, if I lived in either country for any length of time, I daresay I should cease to notice it and get used to jolting along. On the other hand, I believe —and I hope—that I should never become unaware of the disregard for the look of those same streets. Another reason for my not wishing to live in one of these great nations is that they do not, even to the same imperfect degree as the countries of western Europe, make beauty a matter of public concern, nor ugliness of public shame.

In the cities both of America and Russia one is constantly assaulted by the written word. In Russia propaganda slogans are strung across the streets, tied to scaffolding, and draped along the entire front of a block of flats. In America almost

every shop bears strident notices calling attention to its bargains. The slogans and the notices are so numerous that they defeat their own object and one reads none of them, just as one doesn't examine each tree in a forest. They contrive all the same to enforce a general impression of hideousness, somehow disordered and monotonous at the same time. This is partly because they are always in the same colors—white on red in Russia, red on white in America. But the main factor in making the effect so repulsive is that the letters are too big, too thick, too close together, and printed without any thought of design. Lettering is one of the useful arts which matter a good deal to the man in the street (to use this phrase literally for once), and to which some attention is paid in Europe. Neither in America nor in Russia does it seem to exist.

Ever since cars have existed, a running fight has been waged in America about billboards along the roads. Opponents argue, first and foremost, that these advertisements distract the driver's attention and cause accidents, which is certainly true. They also point out that billboards are ugly and deface the countryside, or rather obliterate it in some places. But I doubt if any real campaign could have been mounted against the billboards on this basis alone. The vast billboard put up by a major advertiser is really the lesser part of the nuisance. It consists of a monstrous picture and very few words, and nobody's eye is likely to dwell on it, especially as everyone has seen it countless times already. The sign put up on individual initiative to advertise a local restaurant, real-estate business, or church (no religious body considers that it is duly propagating the Gospel without highway signs) gives all kinds of directions and details and is much harder to evade. If you are what a writer has recently called a sauce-bottle reader—someone who is compulsively drawn to read even the label on a sauce bottle—you can almost succumb to the hysteria of literacy by the end of a day's driving. The serial advertisement, invented by Burma-Shave and copied by other firms, is the most insidious and abominable of all. A message couched in doggerel verse (I don't know why bad verse sticks in the mind more than great poetry; but it does, and the advertisers know it) is divided into fragments, each with its own sign,

spaced over a distance of a quarter of a mile or so. If you read one, the approach of a six-ton truck on the wrong side of the road will not divert you from reading the rest.

At a glance—and a glance is all they will get from the careful driver—Russian billboards look very much like those in America. They are put up with an equal disregard for the countryside, usually at the crown of a hill to blot out the view. The big pictures are the most standardized, and the happy family that has invested in state bonds bears a striking likeness to the happy American family that has bought a new Ford. Other familiar figures are the mother and baby who demand peace; the worker in overalls who pledges himselm to fulfill the plan; and the smiling and patriotic milkmaid, whose face appears beside that of a smiling and patriotic cow (socialist realism is quite capable of making a cow smile) and who is "transforming socialist agriculture." Other tableaux are rather more unexpected. A little Moldavian village through which I passed must be proud of its huge Negro, breaking his chains and scattering imperialists in sun helmets, who announces that "colonialism is meeting its doom."

These billboards are varied by those, which again have their counterparts in America, announcing the distance to a big city, with a saccharin picture of the Kremlin, the hills of Kiev, or (in the case of Odessa) a ship on a blue sea. Within a city, and even on its outskirts, there are no direction signs at all, and the traveler leaving Moscow for Kiev is left to find the road as best he can; but once he is on his way, and unlikely to come to a road junction for fifty miles or so, he is reminded of his destination by a billboard every two miles.

Finally there are the billboards with a great deal of reading matter: either a quotation from Lenin or Khrushchev, an outline of national policy, or a list of the targets in the regional production plan, each calculated to the minutest percentage. I devoutly hope that these billboards are scrutinized only by pedestrians, for any driver who tried to read them would land in the ditch, or on the sidewalk if it is a case of a slogan hung across a city street. As you drive east along a certain street in Kiev, divided by a central strip of greenery, you may read: "Under the leadership of the Party, under the banner of Marxism-Leninism, the Soviet people

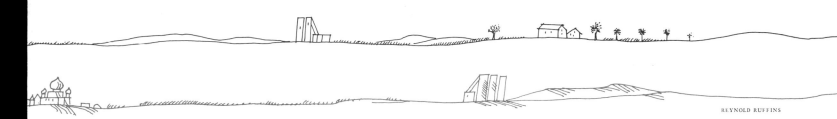

will build a Communist society," As you drive west, the message runs: "The main task of the Party and the Soviet people during the next two decades lies in building the material and technical basis of Communism." This, as it happens, would be a very pretty street if it were left alone.

Aside from making left-hand turns in Moscow (and taking unofficial photographs), I incurred the displeasure of the militia—as the Russian police are called—mainly by giving lifts. I had done this several times without knowing that it was frowned on, when I happened to pick up three men at a main road junction and to be observed by the policemen on duty there. One of these, presumably after making sure of his instructions, pursued me for fifty miles on his motorcycle, flagged me to stop, and said, "I want the Russians." What struck me was that, whereas I argued doggedly until I saw that it was useless, the hitchhikers—who were perfectly capable of knocking the policeman flat, and certainly of sitting tight—meekly got out without saying a word. I last saw them as three dwindling figures standing by the road a long way from nowhere, mute symbols of the Soviet capacity for blind obedience.

Twenty miles farther on, another policeman—no doubt alerted by phone or radio—stopped me and demanded, "Where are the Russians you picked up?" The first man had advanced a variety of specious arguments, such as that I might have had an accident and that the Soviet Union had excellent bus services; this policeman said flatly that foreigners are not permitted to give lifts, and that I ought to have been warned of this at the frontier.

A few days later I gave a lift to a peasant woman and her two sacks of potatoes, which she was going to sell in the market at Odessa, a hundred and fifty miles away. (Comment on an economy in which people go that distance to sell potatoes would surely be superfluous.) She told us that the buses refused to take potatoes and the lorry drivers were under orders not to give lifts. As cars on this road average three an hour, it was hardly astonishing that she had been waiting for seven hours.

Since nobody had seen me stop for her, I thought I was safe this time. I had reckoned without the police check point on the outskirts of Odessa. These check points only occur within a hundred miles or so of the frontiers: between Odessa and Parubnoye there was one at every town. The policeman on duty insisted that the woman get out. When I said that this was ridiculous, and that I might as well take her the last two miles of her journey, he called by radio for his sergeant. The latter, as I might have expected, refused to relent. I allowed myself a few acid remarks on such themes as freedom and brotherhood between the peoples of the world (the latter was extolled on a nearby billboard). In the authentic style of cops the world over, the sergeant replied that he was there to do his job, not to discuss politics. I then expressed the hope that he would help the woman to get a lift in a Russian car, and said I should like to stick around till this happened. To this he said, "I hereby order you to drive on—and don't stop until you report to the Intourist Office." The woman, I need hardly add, said not a word.

This incident had a comical epilogue. Four days later, when I had left Odessa, the policeman at the first check point where I showed my passport and license asked sternly, "Where is the Russian woman you carry with you?"

Somewhere in Kursk province or in Kansas, a bus stops and a man gets out. Taking a dirt road at a strict right angle to the highway, he sets off to walk the miles to his home. The bus rolls on. In a minute he is a speck in a great stillness. He is deep in Russia or in America, deep as one can never be deep in England. He is among people who have never seen the sea or a frontier, never met a foreigner or heard a word of a strange language. I think of him when people ask me what the Russians (or the Americans) think about Berlin or Laos or the Congo. Down the dirt road live the people whose known world is smaller than their country, for whom "the international situation" is beyond knowledge and mostly beyond thought.

But down the dirt road, too, are the sources of a kind of strength that smaller nations cannot achieve. Of either America or Russia, one can say: this country grows all its own food, mines all its own coal, makes all its own iron and steel, has under its soil all the oil and all the important metals it needs. That, ultimately, is why the United States and the Soviet Union are the Big Two.

A Modern Bestiary

Two naturalists identify some fauna from current mythology

A Portfolio by EDWARD SOREL *and* PAUL DAVIS

Classically a bestiary is a medieval moral or allegorical treatise on beasts and their habits. It combines the characteristics of an illustrated natural history text and Aesop's fables, describing the nature and habits of living creatures—both mythical and real—while drawing farfetched lessons from them. ("Because a wolf is never able to turn its neck backwards, except with a movement of the whole body, it means that the devil never turns back to lay hold on repentance.") However lofty the lessons, though, the descriptions of the animals tend to be decidedly earthy.

There are antecedents for the bestiary as far back as the fourth-century *Physiologus,* which in turn grew from the *Hexameron* of Saint Ambrose and other works based ultimately on Aristotle, Herodotus, and Pliny. These chroniclers drew their more-or-less scientific data from oral tradition, mythology, and an irreducible minimum of personal observation. The rarer creatures were all invented, and even the real ones were, as one authority puts it, "splendidly free from the fetters of realism."

With the inexorable march of natural history toward observable truth, the forces of the scientific have come to prevail over those of the imaginative. Broken in rank and dropped from the file are such marvelous beasts as the Manticora ("a lion's body: a tail like the sting of a Scorpion, and a shrill voice. . . . It hankers after human flesh most ravenously") and the Monoceros ("a monster with a horrible howl, with a horse-like body, with feet like an elephant, and with a tail like a stag's. . . . Not a single one has ever come alive into the hands of man"). While we now have a reliable body of zoologic knowledge, as a result there are those who feel that we have paid too great a price in the loss of spirit.

Two of the more retrogressive natural historians working in this field today are the Americans Edward Sorel and Paul Davis. Deciding to restore the bestiary to its former heights of moralizing and inexactitude, Sorel and Davis fixed their unscientific gaze upon some present-day fauna. The following eight pages are the product of an expedition by these two naturalists into the trackless wastes of the current scene, in which they traversed sere savannahs of civic renewal and celluloid swamps, as well as the yet uncharted areas where the Groves of Academe border the Federal Foothills.

Sorel and Davis are young and younger. Sorel, born just before the crash of 1929 (and "nervous ever since," he says), is a native New Yorker and a product of the New York Rapid Transit Academy: Saturday morning art classes as a youngster at the Little Red Schoolhouse in Greenwich Village, followed by the High School of Music and Art and the Cooper Union Art School. By Sorel's own account, he was very talented at twelve and it was downhill from there until his graduation from Cooper Union, whereupon he held and lost eleven jobs in one year. After that nomadic start, Sorel pitched camp for two years at CBS as a designer of promotion material. Free-lancing since 1955, Sorel has written and illustrated children's books as well as a handbook on *How to be President.* He is currently turning into both a book and a musical play his account of the happenings here on earth when the moon is found to be missing. Sorel has left the actual painting of the following portfolio to his friend Paul Davis, while he himself instigated it and contributes to it as writer and moralizer.

Born in Oklahoma in 1938 (Sorel: "*Nobody* was born in 1938!") and raised in Arkansas, Texas, Kansas, and Montana, Davis just knew he "was going to make it as an artist." Son of a Methodist minister and an artistically trained mother, Davis was "always drawing but never saw any art." During the war, the senior Davis was stationed in Alaska as an Air Force chaplain. In their letters, father and son exchanged drawings—Davis remembers with greatest warmth droodles, and sketches of Eskimos. By the time he came East to a scholarship at New York's School of Visual Arts, Davis's artistic stimuli had been specific, limited, and constant—three pictures that traveled with the family back and forth across the American midlands: (1) a woodcut by his mother of an old lady picking rags, (2) a ship under full sail on the ocean, and (3) a hand-colored photograph of a road disappearing into a wood.

Hardly a primitive himself, Davis has reconciled a seemingly contradictory virtuosity with a Plains-plain style. So sophisticated is his handling of the medium—the cracks and flaking of paint are produced at will—that Davis has been approached with the suggestion that he enter the ever-growing market for "genuine" primitives. He declined. There is an openness and honesty in Davis the man that parallel the artist. When asked for his own estimate of the work shown here, he replied: "The best thing I've ever done." IRWIN GLUSKER

The American Bittern

(Aynrandus ferox)

A member of the heron family, generally found in the extreme right of the United States, sometimes called "The Most Bittern" to distinguish it from the ordinary, unheroic "Least Bittern." Unlike latter gregarious variety, does not nest in Birch trees; disdains marshes, bogs, and Goldwaters; and seeks solace at fountainheads in what it imagines are the highest, craggiest peaks. (These sometimes seem mere foothills, intellectually, to many bird watchers, but the Bittern is nearsighted.) Builds large, impressive nest, near which is usually deposited a *mons verborum* (Gr: λογόρροια), or pile of verbiage. When angered, destroys nest and pecks at leftists, loafers, and opponents of *laissez faire*. Motto: "Money is the root of all good." Device: The dollar sign. Utters little glad cries in presence of the Big Rich. Warp worse than woof.

The Painted Bunting

(Taylora plethora)

Linnaeus is credited with making the rosy-breasted, or painted, bunting known to bird lovers—and who, indeed, does not love this bird, save possibly a worry-bird named Spyros Skouras? This Bunting is attractive to many species, especially Nicky Birds, Mickey Birds, and Dicky Birds, during protracted mating season. Moves from nest to nest, trailing its assorted young, but is sometimes bothered by rejected mates. Our painting symbolically represents one of these as a handsome prince turned back into a blues-singing frog. Habitat: the watering places of the world, wherever the photographers of such bird-watching magazines as *Life, Modern Screen, Look,* and *Cosmopolitan* come for crumbs. Feathers by Dior. Body by Fisher.

The Grouper

(Susskindus interminatus)

Generally caught on Eastern networks, where it swells to large dimensions. Easily identifiable by "open end" (in head, just below nose), which emits steady stream of bubbles and, on occasion, bobbles. Produces commercials and attacks on commercials with equal gusto. Plugs Gusto (a condiment), the New York *Herald Tribune,* the classics, culture in all flavors, and self without fear or favor. Like David of the Bible, unafraid of anyone, even Khrushchev, but less adept with slingshot. At spawning time avoids untried waters and produces remakes of television plays which are remakes of movies which are remakes of *David Copperfield.* In late-evening bloating season, known to science as the *colloquium ad infinitum,* can outlast all the stopped watches of the night.

The Pack Rat

(Sinatrus fatuus)

Sleek and impeccably groomed, this rodent travels in packs often called "clans." It is sometimes found preening in Washington, D.C., sometimes fighting at the Stork Club in New York, but most frequently simply playing in Southern California, where the climate works strange mutations in nearly all flora and fauna. Observe that it is feeding time, but that none of the pack will so much as touch a bite—or drop—of its favorite grain derivative until The Leader, or *Sinatrus maximus*, makes the first move; for this is a collective, or mass-culture, animal. As in all primitive societies, the Fuehrer Principle is followed, and the penalty for nonconformism is expulsion; if separated from his "cool" life and forced to live among the "squares" and "Harveys" of the outer "Clyde," or "non-Den" territory, a "gasser" or "broad" soon "takes a

dive." (For technical terms, see Merriam-Webster's new Third International Dictionary.)

Beside the Leader Rat (A), our artist has sketched a Pat's Rat, or *Pee-tah* at (B), since every Pack must have at least one member with links to other prominent clan families or groups, and a Tonyrat (D), a Deanrat (E), and a Joeyrat (unlettered). The smiles are purely habitual, or anticipatory, on the theory that someone, someday, may say something amusing. The Joeyrat has given up, and may be sick—a comic's disease. Presence of Sammyrat (C) and Canary, or MacLaine's, Rat at far left indicates spread of membership. Although the Pack Rat is relatively harmless, it is often set upon by the *Felis gossipa*, or Heddacat (at window in characteristic pose). When the cats lose interest, the Pack may die out, or grow up.

The Sand Hog, or Badger

(Zeckendorfus barbarus)

A burrowing animal, fully webbed and napped except for the sharp claws used in operating its famous game called "urban renewal." In this process the resourceful little creature, equipped with such clever devices as ground leases, accelerated depreciation allowances, mortgage pyramids, and mergers—yet rarely a penny of its own money—can level a city faster than you can say "Robert Moses." Reproduces by subdividing. Approach of its bulldozing claws into hitherto unharmed areas marked by sudden appearance of white X's on windows and shutting off of heat unless taken to court, where it knows everyone anyway. Makes grunting noise that sounds like "Title One! Title One!"; abhors high ceilings, thick walls, and decorative architecture. Naturalists believe it instinctively builds drab buildings the way the beaver builds leaky dams.

The Minnow

(Squalus minimus, or Moby Newt)

Small but dead-game fish known to commercial anglers and networkers as "The Detestable Carp." Carnivorous and herbivorous, attacking the wasteland water snake and octopus as eagerly as it chews at such sedimentary sea growths as Westernweed, Gangsterplant, and Commercial Kelp. Gives off steady glow of indignation visible even in the depths of the Sarnoffo Sea and the Stanton Deep. Has an uncanny ability to spot the hook behind the bait. Armed with sharp but slightly recessed licensing teeth, the Minnow also carries a deadly secretion, or mystery ingredient, called "rampant public interest." On occasion it surfaces and blows just like a whale—and a Right Whale at that. Could the Minnow grow into a whale? The question absorbs Madison Avenue naturalists.

The Barred Owl

(*Arthurus ululus,* or Stately Welfarer)

This ornament to ornithology is widely known as a singer of praises and a viewer-with-alarm. Perches somewhat left of center, especially during egg-laying season. Heavily footnoted. Prodigious moulter of speeches and white papers. Unlike more familiar Wise Old Owl, Loquacious Young Owl prefers the platform to the oak. The more it reads, the more it writes. The more it writes, the greater it swells. A favorite of the keeper in the Washington Zoo, where it likes to perch on the back of his rocking chair, flap its wings, and pretend it is causing all the motion.